Praise for Paul Zane Pilzer

"I'm amazed at your business capacity and, as well, your ability to put into laymen's terms the alchemic process. I know *[Unlimited Wealth]* will be well received and a huge success."
— Sam Walton, Chairman, Wal-Mart Stores, Inc.

"His theory is crystal clear and applicable to anyone...*Unlimited Wealth* is bound to revolutionize the way we view the nation's economy, if not our own lives. Pilzer challenges us to scrap not only the way we think about our daily affairs but the way we prepare ourselves for the future."
— *Newark Star Ledger*

"In *God Wants You To Be Rich*, bestselling author Paul Zane Pilzer provides an original, provocative view of how to accumulate wealth and why it is beneficial to all of humankind. A theology of economics, this book explores why God wants each of us to be rich in every way—physically, emotionally and financially—and shows the way to prosperity, well-being and peace of mind."
— *Boston Herald*

"Paul Zane Pilzer's *God Wants You To Be Rich* makes you understand how and why the world will be getting ever richer materially. He gets it right."
— Julian Simon, Professor of Business Administration, University of Maryland, author of *The Ultimate Resource*

"...*[Unlimited Wealth]* explains how today's billionaires will create their wealth by producing goods and services that did not exist at the time of their birth...a good theory that has implicitly become part of modern economic thinking."
— *National Review*

"*Unlimited Wealth* is as refreshing as a tulip in April. Paul Zane Pilzer has compiled some of the intellectual building blocks that hold expansion theories together...things often lost in the daily exchange of news and information."
— *Detroit Free Press*

"There is much to like in *Unlimited Wealth*. Pilzer's arguments are refreshingly unrooted in any single ideological camp."
— *Washington Monthly*

"It is inspiring to listen and read Paul Zane Pilzer's thoughts—be it in person or through one of his books—because whether it be economics, success principles, attitude or personal health, Pilzer, by his own example, has already put them to work in his own life."
— Don and Jan Held, Independent Business Owners

Other books by Paul Zane Pilzer

The New Health Insurance Solution (2006)

The Wellness Revolution (2002)*

The Next Trillion (2001)*

God Wants You To Be Rich (1995)*

Should You Quit Before You're Fired? (1992)

Unlimited Wealth (1990)*

Other People's Money (with Robert Dietz) (1989)*

* First Edition

THE NEXT MILLIONAIRES

200 Swisher Road
Lake Dallas, Texas 75065
U.S.A.
Toll-free: 800.752.2030
Tel: 940.497.9700
www.VideoPlus.com

VideoPlus is a registered trademark of VideoPlus, L.P.

Printed in the United States of America.

Designed by Momentum Media, a division of VideoPlus, L.P.

THE NEXT MILLIONAIRES

A vast amount of new wealth is being created over the next ten years. Here's why—and how— *you* can be part of it.

PAUL ZANE PILZER

In association with

momentum media

a division of **Video** *Plus*

Contents

Dedication

To those on their way to making our world a better place, and creating extraordinary wealth and joy for themselves in the process.

Acknowledgments

To all those friends and acquaintances I have had the privilege of meeting since first being introduced to the direct selling industry in 1991: from CEOs and top distributors I have come to know well, to those of you for whom I've signed a book or with whom I've stopped to chat at events—you know who you are. I wish I could list every one of you by name, as you've been so important in my life. There is nothing more motivating than to know you are out there, changing the world one person at a time, and to hope that my research helps you do even better what you already do so well. I salute you all.

My thanks to the entire team at VideoPlus, and especially to Stuart Johnson, my friend and advocate, for his unswerving service to the world and his brilliant insights into the direct selling industry.

I am grateful to John David Mann, whom I have respected and admired for years for his gift with language and his commitment to helping people. He has tirelessly helped me cull through more than 5,000 pages and 50 hours of notes and new research, recordings and speeches to help me bring this message to you.

And my extra special thanks to Reed F. Bilbray, my ex-banker, former campaign manager, and lifelong business partner and friend, with whom I've had the pleasure and honor of working every day since he graduated college more than 20 years ago. Reed once again helped to steward a vital project through a maze of deadlines and logistics with his usual unlimited grace and aplomb. Reed, you make it seem so easy!

But most of all, to my wife Lisa and our four children, Miriam, Maxwell, Michael and Mark, who make everything worthwhile.

Foreword

In 1991:

- U.S. household wealth stood at $13 trillion.
- There were 3.6 million U.S. millionaires.

By 2001:

- U.S. household wealth had *tripled*, to $40 trillion.
- The number of U.S. millionaires had *doubled*, to 7.2 million.

From 2006 to 2016:

- U.S. household wealth will reach $100 trillion.
- The exploding U.S. economy will create *10 million new millionaires*.

Will you be one of them?

Introduction

Crisis or Opportunity?

In 1989, at the beginning of the worst period of economic decline since the Great Depression of the 1930s, most experts were predicting decades of economic gloom. The most popular book in the country was titled *The Great Depression of 1990*.

That year, at the lowest point of this recession, I wrote a book that explained why exactly the opposite was true. This book, *Unlimited Wealth,* explained a new theory of how our economy works and made a number of predictions:

- Unprecedented Economic Growth: The longest period of economic expansion in the history of the world was just about to begin, a period of seemingly impossible low interest rates, low inflation and high economic growth.

- Low Interest Rates: I predicted that interest rates would fall to the floor and stay there due to greatly reduced demand for, and increased supply of, money—interest is nothing more than the price of money. Traditional net borrowers (large corporations and many first-time home buyers) were becoming net savers. The newer technology-driven businesses (e.g., Microsoft®) were now growing without needing huge amounts of cash—in fact, they were even *generating* cash as they grew.

- Selective Prosperity: Unlike other periods of economic prosperity, during this time only certain people, industries and economies would prosper. *Unlimited Wealth* claimed that the then-wealthiest per capita economy in the world, Japan, was about to collapse, while the economy of the United States in the 1990s would rise to unprecedented heights.

- The Opportunity in Distribution: The *distribution* of goods and services would become far more important than the production of goods and services; tomorrow's billionaires would make their money *distributing* things rather than by *making* things or controlling natural resources.

- The Internet Opportunity: A new industry (the "Internet") would emerge in the 1990s and it would make information about products and services more valuable than the products and services themselves.

- Incredible Personal Opportunity: Those individuals who understood this new theory of our economy and followed its precepts could accumulate not only millions but also billions just in the decade ahead.

"Pollyanna!" booed some of the critics. "Ridiculous, unfounded optimism," they cried. To some, my 1990 forecasts seemed like pure science fiction.

True, there were some innovative business leaders who praised the book and my theory of "economic alchemy," including Sam Walton, the founder of Wal-Mart and then the richest man in the world. The direct selling community—interestingly, a group that often picks up on trends long before the rest of the world has noticed them—was quick to grasp the significance of *Unlimited Wealth*, and I soon found myself becoming acquainted with this vibrant and growing element of the business world.

> *The direct selling community is a group that often picks up on trends long before the rest of the world has noticed them.*

But for the most part, the general economic community rejected my theory and its predictions for the '90s. In 1991, *Unlimited Wealth* was ridiculed on the editorial page of *The Wall Street Journal*.

The ridicule didn't last long: just five years later, articles praising me and the predictions in my book appeared on the front page of *The Wall Street Journal*. Over the next ten years, people began accepting the economic theories explained in *Unlimited Wealth* as the forecasts proved accurate!

The Economy of the 1990s

From 1991 to 2000, the overall world economy doubled in size, enjoying the highest growth rates ever recorded with the lowest interest rates and lowest inflation. Household wealth in the United States alone tripled to more than $40 trillion. The number of millionaires doubled, from 3.6 to 7.2 million families in the United States alone. The number of billionaires tripled worldwide.

Meanwhile, the Japanese and certain other economies collapsed. And within the countries that prospered, not everyone shared equally in the rising prosperity—but this time, as explained in *Unlimited Wealth,* the choice of who got left out had nothing to do with the color of their skin, their religion, the wealth of their family, or even their education.

And the Internet, of course, emerged as a new trillion-dollar industry; *Time* magazine's 1999 "Person of the Year" was an Internet billionaire whose company did not even exist when my book came out.

Then, everything changed on September 11, 2001.

As the towers of the World Trade Center came crashing down before our very eyes, something else came crashing down along with them. Millions of people lost faith in their economic future, and their belief that they could still shape their economic destiny.

Since "9/11," millions of people and businesses have begun to accept that their temporary economic situation could be permanent. This acceptance is the greatest threat to our way of life—even greater than the physical threat caused by the heinous acts of those responsible for 9/11. For just "as a man thinketh in his heart so is he," in today's modern economy, "as a people think about their economy so is it."

Where Is Our Economy Going Now?

During the 1990s, we witnessed the most unprecedented economic boom in history. With the rise of the Internet, we watched the kinds of changes that used to take place over centuries or decades happen in mere years or even months. We were surrounded on all sides by startling evidence of the limitless abundance that pushes to greet us as we continue to make new discoveries at ever more dizzying speeds, and pushes back the boundaries of human ignorance.

Yet today, in the aftermath of 9/11, many of us seem to have forgotten much of what we have seen with our own eyes. The combination of economic readjustments with the prospect of worldwide terrorism has caused many people, and many leaders, to act like deer in headlights.

In the months immediately following the events of 9/11, our economy understandably took a turn for the worse. Everyone was reeling, both from what had happened and from the implications of what had happened. People were shocked, stunned and worried.

Everyone remembers this. But here is what everyone forgets: in the third quarter of 2001, our gross domestic product (GDP) declined by 0.2 percent, and everyone screamed "Recession!" But the following quarter, the GDP grew again—in fact, by ten times the amount of the decline! Our gross domestic product has risen in every single quarter since. Our economy quickly regained its headlong rush into this new era of increased wealth and prosperity that had begun in 1990; by 2005, even the Dow Jones—the widely regarded and tracked stock market index—had fully recovered. U.S. household wealth rose from $40 trillion in 2001 to $48 trillion by 2005.

While our economy has recovered, most people don't realize it. This too is understandable: people have themselves not recovered emotionally. Sadly, many of them will not only miss out on the extraordinary opportunity offered by the dizzying rate of change this book describes, but they will also unfortunately probably lose their jobs by not being able to react in time.

The Purpose of This Book

The purpose of this book is not to talk about our society, our government or our country's or the world's economic policies. The purpose of this book is to talk about you and your life. About where our economy has been and (especially) where it's going. And most of all, about what you can do, not just to survive, but to thrive and prosper in the years ahead.

During the years from 1991 to 2001, there were more than three and a half million people who refused to be distracted by *The Great Depression of 1990*. Over that decade, these individuals doubled the number of millionaires in the United States by becoming millionaires themselves.

Right now, those exact same conditions apply—*only more so*. And today there arc at least *ten million* more people who will shrug off the pessimism and malaise of the times, who will grasp and ride the surging currents of new wealth creation over the next ten years to become the Next Millionaires.

I invite you to be a part of this group, and in these pages, I will show you how.

Chapter 1

Economic Myths and Realities

Myths and Realities

The introduction to this book is titled "Crisis or Opportunity?" because these are the two prevalent and opposing views that exist today. Which perspective people subscribe to will drive their choices, their actions and, to a great extent, their destinies. My purpose is to give you enough information to see for yourself that the true situation in which we find ourselves is the latter and not the former.

Of course, there are also crises. There is no such thing as a trouble-free world. And I don't want to minimize or ignore the very real suffering and difficulties experienced by the unemployed, the dispossessed and all those who experience loss as they struggle their way through the dizzyingly rapid and often confusing shifts in the patterns of modern life. But the plain truth is that we live in a time of astonishingly rich opportunity.

We will look into each of the issues raised below in greater detail through the course of this book; the purpose in this chapter is simply to introduce the ideas behind these two positions: the myths of crisis and the realities of opportunity.

Myth #1: With dwindling oil supplies, the economy's days are numbered.

The entire economy of the modern world is teetering on the brink of slow extinction because our biggest strength is our biggest weakness, i.e., our complete dependence on oil. It's clear that the planet's supplies of oil are running out, and when they do, the party's over.

REALITY: We will never run out of resources because we always invent new ones.

Since the beginning of human time, when hunter-gatherers roamed from place to place when food supplies were exhausted, we have always been "running out" of resources. Yet every time we reach the limits on one resource, we use our human ingenuity to invent a new and better one.

> *Many often say we have always been "running out" of resources.*
> *Yet every time we reach the limits on one resource, we use our*
> *human ingenuity to invent a new and better one.*

Myth #2: Unemployment is up; the economy's in bad shape.

Ever since the dot-com bust, and especially since 9/11, things have been going downhill in a handbasket. Unemployment's up, growth and opportunity are down. Between the looming threat of international terrorism and the way all our jobs are being siphoned off by cheaper labor in Asian markets, the mood of American business is gloomy, and bound to get only gloomier.

REALITY: Our economy is in the middle of its greatest growth spurt in history.

Except for the brief slowing in the last quarter of 2001, our gross domestic product has increased every single quarter-year since the start of the century. We have picked up where we left off, from the historic decade-long economic expansion of 1991–2001, and are in the first years of another period of extreme economic growth. Unemployment, while it is painful for the workers who are temporarily displaced, is a necessary and positive sign that the economy is growing. In essence, we are disengaging the workforce from less productive businesses to be retrained for work in newer and more productive ones, just as in the twentieth century millions of workers left the farms for the factories, and later left the factories for newer retail industries.

At the same time, this will be a period of highly selective prosperity; that is, only certain people, industries and economies will prosper. This is because the rate of change has become so fast, only those who are quickest to adapt to new technologies and the new markets they represent will be in a position to take advantage of this growth.

Myth #3: The globalization of the economy is wreaking havoc on America.

All the best jobs are going overseas. With China emerging as the world's newest economic superpower and all our information technology (IT) and other high-tech jobs going to places like Singapore and India, our growing unemployment rate is only going to increase.

REALITY: America is leading the way in new and emerging industries.

Every time United States companies move jobs overseas, they do so for one and only one reason: to increase profits. And these added profits don't go overseas—they stay here in the United States, where they create more buying power and more growth. The greatest growth in the economic growth spurt we're now entering will come in new and emerging industries, including Internet services, the burgeoning wellness industry, intellectual distribution and direct selling.

Again, though, there will be an increased disparity during this period of extreme growth. It will not be between America and Asia, or certain population groups and others, so much as between those who involve themselves in the new and emerging growth industries and those who do not.

Myth #4: The Internet is yesterday's news.

The Internet boom has come and gone—if there ever really was one. Or was it all smoke and mirrors? Wasn't that the story with all those dot-com initial public offerings (IPOs) in the late '90s: big expectations, but no real earnings? Looks like maybe the Internet was not all it was cracked up to be.

REALITY: The Internet represents one of the greatest economic revolutions in history—and it's just getting started.

Just as the automobile grew to change the face of modern society, over the coming decade the Internet will spread well beyond its current definitions and applications and begin to permeate every aspect of our lives. The impact of the Internet, which is even now only in its infancy, can only be compared to the invention of writing, which created the birth of civilization, and the printing press, which created industrialization.

> *The impact of the Internet, which is even now only in its infancy, can only be compared to the invention of writing, which created the birth of civilization, and the printing press, which created industrialization.*

Myth #5: Going into business for yourself is risky.

Who can afford to lose out on health insurance and retirement benefits? As everyone's belt gets tighter, it's harder and harder for the home based entrepreneur to compete. The safest, most secure position is to work for a corporation.

REALITY: Maybe two or three decades ago. But in today's world, working for yourself is actually the safer route, and working for a corporation has become the riskier proposition.

Due in part to recent changes in tax law, the principle advantages of being an employee have now become equally available to the self-employed entrepreneur.

And with a sweeping trend toward decentralizing large firms and shifting toward smaller businesses, "virtual corporations" and independent contractors, the individual entrepreneur today is often far more competitive than the big corporation. Entrepreneurs will be the biggest beneficiaries of this economic boom.

> *The individual entrepreneur today is often far more competitive than the big corporation.*

Myth #6: It's harder than ever for the individual entrepreneur to get ahead.

Individual opportunity is shrinking. Small businesses are being gobbled up by large firms, large firms are being absorbed into multinationals, and the Internet is fast making person-to-person businesses, such as direct selling, obsolete.

REALITY: We are now entering the Age of the Entrepreneur.

Not only have changing tax laws leveled the playing field, but also changes in technology have actually tilted that field *toward* individual entrepreneurs, giving them the distinct edge. Home-based businesses are one of the fastest-growing segments in our economy, and that trend will only continue, as the age of the corporation, which began barely a century ago, now gives way to the age of the entrepreneur.

> *Home-based businesses are one of the fastest-growing segments in our economy.*

Among many other forms of entrepreneurial enterprise, the modern direct selling industry is perfectly poised to flourish in this environment and offer unprecedented opportunity to an unprecedented number of people.

The Economic Opportunity Ahead

The twenty-first century we have just begun will be known as the Age of the Entrepreneur. It will be a time when Americans and others from many of the world's capitalist economies will return to their roots of individual family-owned businesses. With this return will come not only enormous personal wealth for those who get there, but also the affirmation and strengthening of moral and family values, as well as personal and societal freedoms that come with owning your own business and controlling your own destiny.

As we enter the final half of this decade, our economy is in only the fifteenth year of a four-decade economic expansion that began in 1991, although many people don't realize it because of the 2001–2004 economic hiccup caused by 9/11.

During the past few years, many companies have proven their roles in this technology-driven expansion. Many are built around new methods of intellectual distribution. Equally important, some of these companies are actually providers of business opportunities themselves, rather than being merely places of employment. At such companies, notably direct selling companies, you can "have your cake and eat it, too" by entering an already established and proven field or industry while still owning your own business.

The Next Millionaires

In 1991, U.S. household wealth was $13 trillion, and there were 3.6 million U.S. households each with a net worth of $1 million or more.

By 2001, U.S. household wealth had risen to an incredible $40 trillion, and the number of U.S. millionaires had doubled.

After the crash of 2001, many people felt they missed their chance to be part of that boom—yet in the four years following 9/11, U.S. household wealth increased by another $8 trillion! In other words, despite all the bad news you were hearing, household wealth grew by another 20 percent! Although as of this writing census figures are not yet compiled to verify this figure, I would project conservatively that in the same period, we added at least another one million new millionaires.

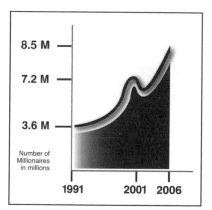

Today, the U.S. and world economies look almost identical to how they looked in 1991, except that there are *more* opportunities for entrepreneurs due to recent changes in taxation and technology.

Based on this history and current conditions, along with other factors that we'll explore in the pages of this book, I now forecast that U.S. household wealth will reach $100 trillion in the next ten years, by 2016—and that *over the same ten years, the exploding U.S. economy will create at least ten million new millionaires.*

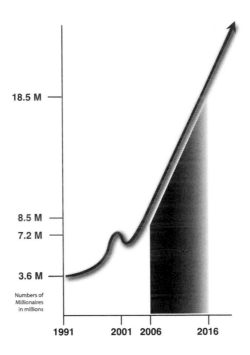

18.5 M

8.5 M
7.2 M

3.6 M

Numbers of
Millionaires
in millions

1991   2001 2006   2016

The Democratization of Wealth

Does that number seem outlandish to you? Are you saying to yourself, "How could we possibly create so many millionaires?!" Then follow this next point:

Over the last few decades, we've seen companies rise from virtually nothing to create huge fortunes. As of this writing, Microsoft has a market cap (value) of $274 billion. If that new wealth were distributed among individuals, a million dollars at a time, it would have created 274,000 millionaires!

By the year 2001, we had a U.S. household wealth of $40 trillion. If we had spread that wealth out, a million dollars per person, how many millionaires do you think that $40 trillion would have produced? *Forty million!*

Of course, Microsoft didn't distribute its wealth to 274,000 individuals, and we didn't spread out our entire $40 trillion in household wealth that way—but the truth is, we're starting to do that more than ever before. The Small Business Association's recent report to President Bush reports that small businesses account for more than one-half our nation's economic output and employ more than half our private-sector workforce—and home-based businesses account for half of small businesses. The large corporation is giving way to the independent contractor and the self-employed entrepreneur.

In effect, we're breaking down those huge corporations into their component parts, namely, the individual entrepreneurs—and as a result, more and more of those entrepreneurs are becoming millionaires. In the past, where we'd see a single company going to $1 billion, today we'll more likely see 1,000 individuals each going to $1 million.

Instead of the rich getting richer, it means there are more people getting rich: the number of millionaires is increasing.

In the past, you never had a chance. Because the big corporation ruled, someone else made that money...the Astors, the Vanderbilts, the Rockefellers. But during the 1990s, 3.6 million people stepped forward and claimed their own fortunes.

Now let's go back to that forecast of $100 trillion in household wealth by 2016. And by the way, that's a conservative forecast. Remember that in the ten years from 1991 to 2001, our household wealth more than tripled, from $13 trillion to $40 trillion. In the next ten years, I'm calling for it only to double, from $48 trillion to $100 trillion.

Where will that new $52 trillion go? Of course, the majority of it will go to make those people who are already wealthy still wealthier. But at least 20 percent of it—$10 trillion or more—will represent new entrepreneurs coming to the table.

That $10 trillion represents ten million new millionaires. The Next Millionaires.

And one of the greatest thrills I have as a writer is knowing that a good number of those Next Millionaires are reading this book right now.

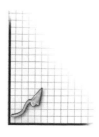

Chapter 2

A Short History of Civilization

Abraham: The First Entrepreneur

As far as we know, the first person in human history who discovered free enterprise, the principle of the entrepreneur, was the prophet Abraham.

Abraham was a nomad from the land of Ur. When he pitched his tent and established his home in Canaan, he discovered that instead of roaming about and taking food off the land, he could become much wealthier if he settled in one place and domesticated animals and planted seeds. By planting food on the land and growing it—in effect, by *making* his own food—Abraham turned from nomad to farmer.

The story of Abraham is the story of a radical transformation from one kind of economy to a wholly different type of economy.

Let's think for a moment about the immensity of what this really means.

A hunter-gatherer wanders over the land, taking food where he can find it and moving on when that piece of land becomes exhausted. That was the economic norm in Abraham's time: most everyone was a gatherer, with tribes going from place to place, forever moving on to the next area of land.

By contrast, farmers identified with and laid claim to a specific piece of land, where they planted seeds and grew a continually renewing supply of food. Because nobody would spend time cultivating land that he or she didn't expect to occupy at the time of harvest, farming is actually predicated on the concept of land ownership.

Rather than going out to scavenge and search out wealth and being dependent upon the land and the weather, Abraham became in charge of *creating his own wealth*. This meant that now, instead of praying, "God, please let me find food tomorrow," he would pray, "God, give me strength and wisdom to plant my food well, wait six months while it grows and then harvest it for the winter."

This was not only a huge economic change, but it was also a social and spiritual shift of seismic proportions.

Abraham is considered the father of the Muslim, Christian and Jewish religions. Abram, his original name, means "father," and Abraham, to which his name was later changed, means "father of many nations." This father of many nations was literally the father of Ishmael (founder of the Arab world) and Isaac (whose direct descendants founded Judaism and Christianity).

But the meaning of this history goes beyond genealogies and biological lineage.

In the Book of Genesis, God promises Abraham, "One day, your descendants will be as numerous as the sands on the shore and the stars in the heaven." But the Hebrew word usually translated as "descendants" is more accurately translated as, "the people who believe what you believe." The "descendants of Abraham" really refers to all *those people who believe in the capacity to create their own wealth, instead of scavenging for it or fighting and killing each other for it.*

And that is an excellent definition of the modern entrepreneur!

> *Modern entrepreneurs are those people who believe in the capacity to create their own wealth, instead of scavenging for it or fighting and killing each other for it.*

The Beginning: The Theory of Economics

Abraham wasn't simply the father of certain ethnic or religious populations. He was also the father of the modern world, in that he came up with the economic model on which we have based the entire development of civilization.

Today, it's easy to take this notion for granted as "normal," but in Abraham's day, it was a radical concept. Imagine how hard it must have been for others to grasp: that instead of having wars and killing each other and hunting the land for the food God put there, you should stay put, own your own land, and grow your own food. To Abraham's neighbors, it must have seemed like lunacy.

Imagine a Philistine from the north or an Egyptian from the south coming upon his land and saying, "Wow, look at all this food growing on this beautiful field. Hey, let's take some of this food and bring it back to Philistia or to Egypt."

And Abraham would come running out in his robe, his beard flying, and shout, "Hey, excuse me! I planted this food—you can't just take it, these are my crops, this is my field."

What would they answer back to such an assertion? "Don't be ridiculous! You can't 'own' land. Nobody 'owns' lands, and nobody 'makes' food. God makes food—everyone knows that! We have every bit as much right to take it as you do."

Can you imagine Abraham trying to argue that he had planted it all six months earlier? They'd think he was crazy.

This is a pattern we'll see repeatedly in the history of free enterprise: innovation and advancement, met with resistance and incomprehension. It's still with us today.

What Abraham wanted more than anything else was for everyone to understand what he had learned: that if we turn to our higher spiritual being—God, or whatever name you want to use for a higher deity or spiritual reality—for knowledge and strength to go and make our food, not to simply have it given to us, then we are capable of unlimited wealth. Abraham realized how prosperous all of God's children could be if everyone strove to create and improve their own property, instead of crossing over the borders and trying to seize property from others by force.

The rest of the world's history is comprised of the more than 5,000 years it has taken us finally to reach that point.

> *What Abraham wanted more than anything else was for everyone to understand what he had learned: that if we turn to our higher spiritual being—God, or whatever name you want to use for a higher deity or spiritual reality—for knowledge and strength to go and make our food, not to simply have it given to us, then we are capable of unlimited wealth.*

Free Trade and the Genesis of Wealth

Today, instead of it being a piece of land, it may be a business, yet the principle is exactly the same. The individual person has his or her property, through which he or she transforms his or her efforts into growth and production. Today's entrepreneurs create wealth by starting with the property they own and then utilizing creativity and technology to create more resources than presently exist.

The idea of entrepreneurial ownership, the principle of Abraham, is what has fueled the economic growth—slow at first, but constantly picking up speed—of the past several thousand years. And it has done so hand in hand with a second powerful economic force: trade.

With ownership came an accelerated drive to innovate, develop, refine and perfect. When you stay in one place and begin to improve the same piece of land, year after year, instead of moving around continually from place to place, the human capacity to invent and improve kicks into high gear. Using our brains and opposable thumbs to make ever better tools, property ownership created new opportunities to develop new tools and new skills.

When we were all hunter-gatherers, we each had the same general skill set. We were all "jacks of all trades and masters of none." But as we became landowners and settled into communities, we began to individuate and each develop our own skills, which led inevitably to ever-increasing trade.

The more we invent and specialize, the more we develop our own unique skills and produce, the more we need to trade with others for their unique skills and produce. Greater and greater diversity of skills, greater and greater specialization, leads to more and more trade. Increased trade leads to a further increase in wealth for all involved.

> *Greater and greater diversity of skills, greater and greater specialization, leads to more and more trade. Increased trade leads to a further increase in wealth for all involved.*

In fact, the only true limit to the wealth of an overall economy is how many people are available for them to trade with. This is why merchants and traders have always been the wealthiest people: they bring specialized produce from one place to another, creating added value by virtue of the trade itself.

Here is a summary of how this process unfolds:

- The more any one of us specializes in one task, the greater our individual output. The more you do one thing, one business, one industry, the better and better you get at that one thing.

- The greater and more specialized your work output, the more you want and need to trade with others for their different and unique output. You find other people to work with, starting with other individuals in your community, then in the next state, then in the next country and eventually the entire world.

- The greater the economic production of a whole society, state or government, the more you need to trade with another state or government for their specialized production. And the more societies with whom you trade, the greater the total global wealth.

From an economic standpoint, that explains the history of the world—and not only economically but socially and culturally, too—because it happens that there is a social fringe benefit to all this trading. The growth of trade and a diversifying economy means we have to learn to get along with more varieties of people, more religions, more cultures and more different ways of looking at the world.

Once you realize that the amount of wealth we can create is limited only by how many people we're willing to trade with, and that in order to trade with more people, we have to be willing to understand and trust more people, you start to cross the line from economics into theology. Because you start to realize that only some higher intelligence, some kind of benign, beneficent being or force, could have created such an unlimited economy based on such a simple yet powerful and loving concept:

Our wealth is rewarded directly in proportion to the number of people with whom we are willing to share.

The Globalization of Free Enterprise

In ancient times, people very quickly figured out that the more roads they built, the more people could shuttle messages and trade goods back and forth. The more roads they built, the more people they could include in their trading block, and the more people could specialize and expand the range and diversity of overall goods and services available, which in turn increased the possibilities for trade.

This is the impulse that led people to live in cities, and it is why societies that wanted to build huge economic power built roads and established trade routes. This is why the Roman Empire covered Europe with a network of marble highways, and why the British Empire established shipping routes all over the world.

If there was one item in the twentieth century that fueled the economic might of the United States and distinguished it from the economic power of its rival, the Soviet Union, it was the massive system of roads it had built in the first half of the century. That highway system, in turn, was itself simply a natural expression of the uniquely powerful element of free trade that was built into this nation at its inception.

The economic power of the United States that became evident during the twentieth century actually stems from a provision in the U.S. Constitution, which said that each state could make its own laws governing its own citizens, could print its own currency, could even have its own army—but no state could create any laws restricting free trade with any other state.

This was a radical thing to do: to tell more than a dozen independently self-governing entities that none of them could stop their consumers from buying from any of the others. This was the first document in history to create such an economic system, and it showed a brilliant and prescient economic understanding on the part of the farmer-entrepreneurs who framed the Constitution.

Today, schoolchildren are taught that freedom of religion and freedom of speech were what the founding of the United States was all about. But as with the story of Abraham, there was something very practical at the heart of this: the founding fathers knew economic persecution as much as (or even more than) any religious persecution. And they understood that true growth would come only from a system that allowed entrepreneurs to freely trade with other entrepreneurs, for the mutual betterment of all.

> *The founding fathers understood that true growth would come only from a system that allowed entrepreneurs to freely trade with other entrepreneurs, for the mutual betterment of all.*

In the modern era, this is no longer an exclusively American phenomenon. The economic power of what we call the Western world is based on the same principles of free trade between its citizens. The billion or so individuals in our free-trading block are so wealthy because every one of them is working at producing their products or services better, or else someone else in that billion-person trading block will.

If you had to summarize what's wrong with the world today, it is that in a world of about six billion people, only about one quarter are engaged in free trade around the world, from Japan to North America to Europe. This is why these are the wealthy people of the world—the "haves." What is it that these one and a half billion people have that the other four and a half billion people do not? Free trade: the ability to produce something and share it freely without their governments suppressing their actions.

The challenge is how to bring the other four and a half billion people of the world into this free trade environment, while at the same time preventing the political instability that often results from rapid change. But difficult though it is, it is inevitable: the clock cannot be turned back, and technology will not slow down nor turn around and develop backwards.

Meanwhile, the engine of creativity, innovation and economic growth that drives this inexorable momentum toward universal freedom of trade and its resulting freedoms of worship, speech and lifestyle, is picking up speed—and those of you reading these pages are uniquely well positioned to be at the heart of that acceleration.

Chapter 3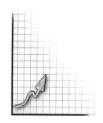

The Economics of Scarcity

Tunnel Vision

The great third-century Christian theologian, St. Augustine, was once asked, "What did God do before he created the universe?" He replied, "He was busy creating Hell for people like you who would ask such questions."

Today, we not only ask such questions, we encourage them. We assume that we deserve every answer. We encourage our children to ask questions we couldn't possibly answer, and to go to school, study, innovate, investigate and find the answers. We *assume* the answers are there to be found—because we now universally recognize that's one of the reasons we're here on earth.

But even when we earnestly look for knowledge, sometimes the very nature of our questions blinds us to possible answers. This is the kind of tunnel vision that handicaps the classical view of economics and haunts us today.

Let me give you an example of what I mean by tunnel vision.

Nearly 2,500 years ago, while Alexander the Great was attempting to create an economic empire by force, his contemporary Aristotle was engaged in transforming the world through technology.

One of the most critical, vexing problems in the agricultural world since Abraham was the challenge of finding a way to predict accurately the seasons, so farmers could maximize their crops. People knew there were cyclic alternations of hot and cold, wet and dry, but entire civilizations had struggled to find a way to make specific sense out of it. They observed the planets meandering in odd, unpredictable courses through the sky (the Greek word "planet" means "wanderer"), and sensed there were complex relationships between the movements of these heavenly bodies and conditions on the earth. But they couldn't come up with a consistent, logical way of accounting for the passage of time.

Aristotle, in observing the heavens, might have said, "Hey, those aren't gods, they're gigantic rocks, and they're each in a fixed orbit around the stationary earth." He worked out an extraordinarily brilliant calendar system based on a year of 12 months and 365 days, which people then used to predict the seasons and trade winds, to administer their farming and bring order to their lives.

And here's the amazing part of it: even though we still use Aristotle's calendar today, it's not really accurate! Why not? Because it's based upon a completely false supposition, namely, that the planets orbit around the earth. (This is why we have to add leap years.)

So problems continued with the calendar. About every 100 years, it would snow in July, and they'd crank the calendar back six months by papal decree, which led to a 500-year quest by astronomers for the perfect calendar.

At the heart of this quest lay a problem that prevented its own solution. The problem lay in the nature of the question: astronomy was the study of how all the planets revolve around the earth. The very definition of the problem precluded anyone coming up with the right answer. The answer lay outside their field of vision: their science was rooted in what we today would call *wrong presuppositions.*

It was tunnel vision.

It wasn't until the Polish astronomer Copernicus proposed that the earth (along with the other planets) actually revolved around the sun that we began to find a viable way of "fixing" Aristotle's work by turning it on its head. Eighty years later, the Italian scientist Galileo used his newly invented telescope to demonstrate that Copernicus was right.

But Galileo had a problem—actually, to the establishment, he *was* a problem. His findings upset the existing paradigm. He was tried and condemned to burn at the stake before he finally recanted. Even though the pope of the time had been Galileo's college roommate and good friend, he could not allow their existing view of the world to be so disrupted.

And in case this sounds like no more than a history lesson, consider this: it wasn't until 1992 that the office of the pope officially reversed its position and extended to Galileo a posthumous apology!

The kind of tunnel vision that said the planets revolve around the earth, that declared the earth was flat, that proclaimed Abraham nuts to try and "own" and cultivate land—is alive and well and with us today, crippling the prevalent understanding of wealth and the economy.

> *The kind of tunnel vision that said the planets revolve around the earth, that declared the earth was flat, that proclaimed Abraham nuts to try and "own" and cultivate land—is alive and well and with us today, crippling the prevalent understanding of wealth and the economy.*

The common view of wealth today, both to laymen and economists, is the equivalent of saying that the planets revolve around the earth. Unless we completely turn our existing paradigm of wealth on its head, like Aristotle's calendar, we have no hope of understanding how our society is changing. And if we do make that change—if we have the courage to put the sun at the center and see things as they really are—then the confusion disappears. Like Galileo looking through a telescope, we find that things become clear: we understand what's going on and how we can make the smartest economic decisions.

The "Dismal Science"

The fatally flawed, "pre-Copernican" worldview that still clouds our economic vision today can be summed up in one word: *scarcity*.

President Harry Truman was once listening to a highly respected economist go on and on about the economic condition of the country. Just as he thought the man had finished making his laboriously complex point, the economist took a breath, and then went on: "On the other hand…"

Whereupon Truman uttered his famous comment, "What this country needs is a good one-handed economist."

It's a funny story, but it points to an underlying tragedy.

Listen to any political debate, in any country, about what measures it will take to help the economy. If this is supposed to be a science, why does it seem like even the scientists haven't the faintest idea which ideas will really work? Why don't they seem to have any answers? Is it science or guesswork?

For most of us, economics is actually the most important science in our lives, in a very tangible way. It is the science that dictates the overwhelming majority of our daily lives and deals with what are often the most vexing and challenging issues of our lives. And here's the amazing thing about that: most people, including most economists, still don't really know what's going on!

Economics today is where medicine was 200 years ago: it has its medicines and procedures, and they sometimes appear to work (although they sometimes kill the patient in the process), but there is no clear theory to explain why they work or don't. We are without a working theory to explain what we see happening around us.

> *Economics today is where medicine was 200 years ago. We are without a working theory to explain what we see happening around us.*

The reason I decided to become an economist is that throughout my childhood, everywhere I looked, it seemed to me that the most pressing issues everyone faced were economic. By learning everything I could about economics, I hoped I would find some keys to helping people learn to better control their lives. In fact, economics is not simply about currency or finances; economics is really the search for controlling our own destiny.

But that's not the way it's traditionally looked at. The traditional science of economics (often called "the dismal science") is the study of scarcity. Look it up in any textbook. "Economics is the study of society's allocation and distribution of scarce resources."

Economics says, "There's a limited supply out there of land, fresh water, minerals and other vital resources; how we divide them up among ourselves is economics." Whether it's communism, socialism, capitalism or any other "ism," it's about taking a fixed supply of resources and "fairly" dividing them up among the population. Implicit in this definition is that, if we're dealing with a fixed supply of resources, the only way we're going to get ahead is by taking it from someone else.

All my work over the past three decades has revolved around the task of debunking the myth of scarcity; in my professional life, there is no greater mission.

> *All my work over the past three decades has revolved around the task of debunking the myth of scarcity.*

Despite our many great gains throughout history, this core idea that we are running out of everything has held our thinking hostage for thousands of years. Today, when there is more evidence than at any other time in history that this idea is wrong, it continues to hold our thinking hostage. That critical and tragic error in perception is at the core of so much misunderstanding and human suffering.

Yesterday's Wars, Today's Terrorism

When you begin with an assumption of scarcity, it's not hard to see where this thinking soon leads. If there is limited supply, what do you do when you are running out? You go next door, kill the people in the next village and take theirs. That is the history of war. It's dressed up with all sorts of rhetoric, justification and complexity, but it really boils down to that.

The entire twentieth century was about fighting over which system is the right system to divide our limited, finite, scarce, fixed wealth. That's what all our wars have really been about. That's what all wars are really about.

Yet we also learned a clear and vivid lesson in the twentieth century. (At least, we learned it to an extent; whether or not we have entirely learned how to put it into practice is another issue.) This lesson is that we have a proven antidote to war: free trade.

> *We have a proven antidote to war: free trade.*

As we've seen, the great economic powers of the Western world derive their wealth and economic might from the practice of relatively unfettered free trade, a model that the United States pioneered and that is now practiced throughout about one-quarter of the world's population.

In addition to hugely multiplying all our wealth, the fact that we are all interdependent on one another economically has also provided a wonderful fringe benefit: it has kept these countries from going to war with each other.

In the decades immediately after World War II, both Germany and Japan quickly became vigorous trading partners with the United States; soon they were major economic powers themselves. Not only did this contribute greatly to the world economy, it also contributed greatly to world stability. There is no way the United States could ever go to war with Germany or Japan again, now that our citizens are such deeply entrenched mutual trading partners.

Perhaps more than any other two countries in the world, Canada and the United States should have long ago gone to war. We have all the classic features of being natural enemies. We share an enormous border. Canada used to be owned by England, with whom we went to war for our independence. Why don't we go to war with Canada? Because our economies has been so intertwined from the start that it would have been impossible. Our people are always on the phone talking to each other. If I told you stories about "those evil Canadians," you wouldn't believe me.

War drives its power from people's fears and ignorance of each other. When we trade with other people, we create bonds that are very difficult to tear apart. Governments wage war, but people create peace, and they do it through a shared economy.

What about global terrorism? Although it feels new to many of us in America, the truth is that there is really nothing new about it. The world has always been susceptible to the grip of terrorism, and although it has had many faces, names and political or religious agendas, it is really always about the same thing: the desire to resist change and hold onto an established order.

What do today's terrorists want, ultimately? They want to prevent the world from changing. They don't want modern ideas of free speech, religion and democracy challenging the order that existed in their lives before. They don't want their children watching American movies or being faced with the challenges of modern, pluralistic thinking.

Just as the church in Galileo's time felt it needed to squash anyone who claimed the planets didn't revolve around the earth, international terrorists today want to kill any person or civilization that threatens to tell their children the world is different from the way they want to continue seeing it.

What is the answer? The answer of Abraham. Entrepreneurship, innovation and free trade.

In fact, one of the reasons our own country has fallen into lower esteem among the other countries of the world lately is that during the 1990s, we retreated economically inward. We focused on America and pulled back on our trading, lending and economic exchange with other nations. We let countries like Afghanistan fall off the map, and stopped building roads and bridges for destitute peoples. In the years to come, we will have to resume our past gregarious ways and reopen more economic pathways to the other countries of the world.

Free trade is the engine that fuels the growth of wealth—and it is also salve to the wounds of war and the source of those bonds that will tie us together in a world with an ever-diminishing impulse to resort to armed hostility.

> *Free trade is the engine that fuels the growth of wealth.*

The problem is we have to look beyond our habitual thinking and see things as they really are.

Look up. Isn't it obvious that all the planets revolve around the earth?

Look at yourself. Isn't it obvious that as you age, your health will naturally start breaking down?

Look around you. Isn't it obvious that we are running out of fuel, land, water and air?

Of course. They're all obvious. But none of them is true. The planets revolve around the sun—earth included. There is no reason we can't grow healthier as we age, if we know how to take care of ourselves and have the resources to do so. And we are not running out of anything—never have, never will.

So much that's obvious is obviously wrong.

Our science caught up with that first reality, astronomy, several hundred years ago. It has just been catching up with that second reality, health and wellness, over the past decade or two. And catching up with the third? We're working on that.

Chapter 4

The Economics of Abundance

When I first began to study economics 30 years ago, I found it incredibly upsetting.

I could not believe that God would create a world of a fixed supply, a world of limited land, minerals, fuels and other resources, a world where we would inevitably have to fight amongst ourselves to determine who gets the most.

No wonder they called it "the dismal science." I just could not accept it.

In 1973, while I was going to college, we had a huge gasoline crisis. Embargoes by the Arab oil-producing nations threatened to collapse our Western economies by sharply limiting our supplies or greatly increasing the prices. Suddenly there was no oil; for a short time, we had gasoline rationing, with long lines at the fuel pumps all across America. Tempers flared, violence simmered and the country sat breathless, waiting, worried.

I watched. What I saw fascinated me.

The average American car at the time got about nine miles to the gallon. Within a decade we had retooled our cars, switching from using mechanical carburetors (which cost about $300 apiece) to computerized electronic fuel injectors (costing about $25), so that they were getting 22 miles per gallon. This change in technology more than doubled our fuel mileage while more than halving the pollution emitted.

In effect, this *doubled* our oil supply.

It was clear to me that there was something going on here, something that conventional economics could not account for. It was clear to me that we needed a new theory of economics.

Theologically, I couldn't accept the traditional economic view that we lived in a world of scarcity that led inevitably to conflict and war. And practically, the evidence around me told a different story.

I could see that somewhere, somehow, we had found a system that lets us create wealth. We don't want to go take wealth from someone else. We want to create new wealth that didn't exist before. This is an enormous paradigm shift, and it's one that we need to embrace—because *it changes everything.*

I could see that ownership coupled with free trade creates a force that transforms competition from a destructive force into a force that works for the betterment of all. That's a just and beneficent God in action. That's an economic theory I could accept.

> *Ownership coupled with free trade creates a force that transforms competition from a destructive force into a force that works for the betterment of all.*

My life's work has been to find a theory of economics that can explain to people everywhere how their economy works—and more importantly, what you individually can do today to accumulate wealth and achieve the balance you seek between your personal and professional lives. That theory is Economic Alchemy.

Economic Alchemy

Although people often think of them as charlatans who monkeyed around with chemicals in a vain effort to make gold, the original alchemists were in reality far different from the popular mythology.

These early Christians, from the first through tenth centuries, were men of profound faith who believed in the ultimate beneficence of God's economy. As representatives of this faith, they believed that through the right combination of prayers, incantations and pureness of heart, the correct mixing of the elements of the natural environment would yield something of far greater value. Were they after gold? Of course not. They were after peace and prosperity for all. Because in those days, the alternative was to take your army, go next door and kill your neighbor for his gold.

The alchemists' formula for creating wealth was about 10 percent scientific formula and 90 percent prayer. For they believed that a true and just God would give us the ability to create wealth.

What is especially interesting about the alchemists is that *they were successful.*

No, they never actually made gold. Instead, their explorations and innovations laid the foundations for modern metallurgy, chemistry, engineering, physics, pharmacy, medicine—all of the sciences that have given us the ability to create unlimited wealth by creating unlimited resources. Today, modern science has given us exactly what the alchemists sought: the ability and opportunity to create unlimited wealth and prosperity for all.

Traditional economic theory is based on scarcity. My new economic theory is based on abundance. I called it "Economic Alchemy" out of respect for and in deference to the ancient alchemists who were the first people with the faith to believe that we had the ability to create unlimited wealth.

In this chapter, I want to give you an understanding of the six laws of economic alchemy; and as we go through them one by one, I want you to keep this question in mind: *How can I see this principle operating in my own life?*

The First Law

Resources are unlimited because our minds are unlimited.

The first law of economic alchemy says that there are no resources to run out of, because all resources are inventions of the human mind.

People are always saying we're always running out of water, running out of land, running out of oil, running out of something…but we never have and we never will. There's nothing to run out of! Why not? Because everything we call a "resource" is simply an invention, a definition of the mind, and before we run out of one, we always define a new one. Resources are unlimited because our minds are unlimited.

Five thousand years ago, oil was a terrible black substance that polluted the water. It was dangerous: slip and fall into oil, and you die. Today, we consider it a valuable resource—in fact, many are bemoaning our fate and predicting the death of the modern economy because we are about to run out of oil.

But history tells a different story.

Although we consider oil the most vital resource today, 150 years ago, it was coal and whale oil, as it had been for centuries. By 1850, we had become extremely efficient at harvesting whales by using gigantic whaling ships that harvested them out at sea, instead of bringing them back to harbor. We had grown so efficient, in fact, that we were harvesting more than 10,000 whales a year from the Atlantic Ocean, and very nearly extinguished the species.

In 1859, William Jevons, then England's greatest economist, was knighted by the queen of England for writing *The Coal Question,* which predicted that the British Empire would collapse by 1900 because it would run out of coal. Of course, Jevons was right: it did run out of coal. But it didn't matter, because by then England had switched to petroleum. The same year that saw publication of Jevons' dire prediction, a retired train conductor named Edwin Drake drilled the first oil well in Pennsylvania.

A little over a century later, a group called "The Club of Rome" wrote a book strangely reminiscent of Sir Jevons' tract. The 1971 *Limits to Growth* predicted that we would run out of oil in 20 years and forecast the demise of the modern way of life. Today, 35 years later, people are now saying we'll run out of oil in 90 years.

This is an age-old theme; it just doesn't reflect reality. We aren't "running out" of resources: there are no "resources" to run out of, because we're constantly defining and inventing new ones.

Whether oil "runs out" in 20 years or 90 years is not the point; we're about to replace all of our carbon-based fuels, which also happen to pollute the air, with hydrogen. I believe we're a perhaps a decade away from having the technology to use this unlimited fuel source.

I know many are skeptical about such a prediction; it could hardly be otherwise. That's the very definition of "innovation." Nobody believed in an oil economy when Mr. Jevons was promoted to *Sir* Jevons. Nobody expected that a $25 fuel injector would replace a $300 carburetor and double our supply of oil by doubling the efficiency with which we use it. They laughed at Abraham.

Land is perhaps the most fought-over resource in history. Yet to our hunter-gatherer ancestors, or to the Native Americans who preceded the Europeans in the United States, land was not a resource. The resource was wild game; land was simply where you ventured to find the animals you hunted and the plants you gathered. When they were gone, you moved on to new land. Just as pre-industrial people had no way of refining oil to use it as a resource, hunter-gatherers had no way of "refining" land, by planting seeds and domesticating animals—the act that distinguished Abraham's career.

Throughout history we have always been about to run out of a resource just before we discovered a new one. And that's no accident: it's why we discover the new one.

All the resources we think we're running out of are really inventions of the human mind—and there is no limit to the human mind.

The Second Law

Technology determines the supply of any given resource.

"Okay, I can accept that over time, we invent new resources—but I've got to run a business and feed my family today, using the resources we know about today. How do I increase my immediate wealth in the practical, right-now world?"

Fair enough. This is where the second law comes in.

The second law says that the supply of any given resource, at any given moment, depends upon the technology with which you find it, extract it and use it.

We already saw an example of this in the new technology of electronic fuel injection that more than doubled our supply of oil in the 1970s and early '80s. Let's look a little closer at that scenario.

Although the fuel injector did multiply our effective fuel supply by increasing how efficiently we used it, that was not the factor that put an end to the lines at the fuel pumps. The reason we stopped having gas lines is that we built a pipeline to Alaska through Canada that made new supplies of oil available. Before this event, this was considered technologically impossible.

What's more, in 1970 we defined "oil" as "oil that exists a mile or less underground." By 1980, our technology had advanced and changed that definition: now "oil" meant "oil that exists *eight* miles or less underground." Soon we refined the technology to do offshore drilling and enlarged that definition yet again. Notice that nothing about our physical world has changed here: it's the *technology* that keeps changing and allowing us to have more resources.

And in case you're thinking of dying otters and the *Exxon Valdez* and all the environmental problems involved in the Alaskan pipeline and offshore drilling, notice something else: as our technologies become more and more efficient, they also become cleaner and cleaner. Coal is a far dirtier resource than oil, and takes a terrible toil in human suffering. The fuels that replace oil will be cleaner and kinder to the environment, too; it's simply the nature of the mind.

THE FORMULA FOR WEALTH

If you need more of any given resource—oil, land, water, minerals—an economist will tell you to start counting how much currently exists and look at our rate of consumption. If there's not enough (and to a traditional economist, there never is), the answer is inevitable: go next door and take it, by trade, persuasion or force.

The first and second laws of economic alchemy render that thinking utterly backwards. It is not the pure physical "resource" that determines wealth, but the innovation and creation of the human mind. Like beauty, wealth quite literally exists in the mind of the beholder.

There is an equation that explains this:

$$W = P \times T$$

Wealth (W) equals the physical resources available (P) multiplied by the technology available (T).

This equation is the heart of my life's work, and it's important that you understand it. Don't worry, it has nothing to do with mathematics: it's pure common sense.

Whether we're talking about the wealth of a nation or your individual wealth, the measure of that wealth will be determined by the physical resources available, magnified by how much technology there is available to find it, extract it and make more efficient and productive use of it.

In our examples above, the P refers to the physical amount of existing oil. And here's the amazing thing: *that amount remained constant.* At no point did we ever actually create more oil. But we created fuel injectors, deeper drilling methods, offshore drilling and the Alaskan pipeline. All of these were changes in T, or technology, and they all acted as multipliers, causing that constant P to generate greater and greater W, or wealth.

Let's apply the equation to land.

Up until the early 1900s, the United States grew as a nation by absorbing more land into its borders. We added our last continental state, Arizona, in 1912. After we dug ourselves out from under the Great Depression, our wealth grew more rapidly and enormously than ever before—yet unlike most growing economies in history, we did so without adding, seizing or claiming any more land. How was this possible?

We grew richer not by taking more land, but by increasing the efficiency with which we used our existing land. While our P remained constant, we multiplied our T.

In 1930, 30 million of the 100 million U.S. population were farmers, and those 30 million struggled to feed all 100 million people.

In the 50 years from 1930 to 1980, the farm population dwindled from 30 million to only three million—to just a tenth its former size. Meanwhile, the country's total population tripled, growing to nearly 300 million. Imagine: three times the number of people to feed, with only a tenth the number of people to do it, and absolutely no increase in the amount of available land. "What an awful recipe for mass starvation!" the traditional economist might say.

But look at how we were doing in 1980: those three million farmers were now feeding 300 million people, and doing it so well that they made an extra 50 percent more food they could sell around the world. America had become known as the "breadbasket to the world."

What changed? Technology. Over those 50 years, we increased our productivity per farmer by 4,500 percent, and productivity per acre of farmland by 1,000 percent, so that one-tenth the number of people could feed three times the population and still have tons left over.

Remember Grandpa's advice? "Land's the best investment; they're not making any more of it." Turns out, it's not really true. By increasing productivity per acre ten-fold, America "created" 100 times more land.

A TALE OF TWO NATIONS

When I was a child, I remember being told my father had come from Russia, and I would look at a map to see what the Soviet Union looked like. It was huge: it stretched from one end of the map to the other. I remember being told, "The Soviet Union is so powerful, because it has the most land in the world, the most fresh water in the world, and the most oil in the world."

The Soviet Union had the lock on P, physical resources. By the old way of thinking, they should have been the wealthiest nation in the world, and should have become the most powerful nation in the world. What happened?

When I was growing up, right after World War II, there was also a certain tiny little island country that was incredibly poor. They had no land, they had no fresh water, and they didn't have a drop of oil. What happened?

What happened was that Japan went on to become the wealthiest per capita country in the world—and the Soviet Union become so poor it imploded and ceased to exist.

It's astonishing: the country with virtually zero resources became the economic powerhouse, while the nation with the most resources disintegrated. Why? Because wealth is no longer about resources—it's about technology. W equals P times T, and the T is now what matters.

Japan led the world in technology, and the Soviet Union, despite its massive resources, couldn't simply conquer people and make them work without technology. It didn't matter if it conquered another republic and claimed it as a part of the empire. You can seize people's land, you can seize their oil, but you can't seize their mental abilities to work their technology.

Today it looks like China is emerging as tomorrow's richest nation in the world. Is that because of their huge land mass and population? Of course not; it had all that land and population for centuries. What's changed is that China has just recently started to adopt the principles behind free enterprise (the secret of Abraham) and discovered how to increase its technology. China is an emerging powerhouse because of technology, not resources.

The Third Law

The advance of technology is determined by the exchange of information.

Once we understand that the key letter of the equation is T, and that the key to increasing our wealth is to acquire more technology, the question becomes, "How do we get more technology?"

In order to get more physical resources, we can take an army and go kill the people next door, then simply take their land, oil or gold. But we realize now that we don't want that stuff, because we'll just end up like the Soviet Union. We want more *technology*. How do we get it? What controls the advance of technology?

This is where the third law of economic alchemy comes in.

The advance of technology is determined by the speed with which you exchange information. The faster we exchange information, the faster we can advance technology. This is one of the secrets to the power of free trade: any system that makes free trade possible also promotes exchange of information—and vice versa.

Ten thousand years ago, the written word created civilization. It didn't just *record* civilization, it *created* it. Before the written word, we had oral traditions, but these were inexact and could pass on only limited amounts of technical information. Writing greatly accelerated and amplified the rate of information exchange.

With the written word, suddenly I could learn a new farming technique, write it down and pass it on, not just to my neighbors, but also to someone who might not even be born yet. I could pass it to my children's children's children. The written word is what fueled the innovations and inventions of entrepreneurial free-trade civilization and spread them around the world.

The printing press created the Industrial Revolution—again, it didn't simply *record* it, it *created* it. With the printing press, I could describe the way I had figured out to make a new loom in England, write it down and ship it over to the United States so it could be duplicated there. The printing press is what enabled an Italian scientist named Galileo to build upon work written 80 years earlier in a different country, by a Polish scientist named Copernicus.

The printed word *accelerated information exchange.*

The same thing that happened with writing and printing is happening now with the computer. The computer was invented only 50 years ago, in 1945. It began to enter our lives as individuals only about 1980, and even then, it hadn't yet become an *information-sharing machine.* In the 1980s, computers were all about spreadsheets and word processors.

In the 1990s, the computer suddenly burst upon the world as a new way to *share information.* Today, the computer and the Internet are accelerating the rate of information exchange at a dizzying speed, and are about to ratchet up civilization, technology and wealth over the next one or two decades at a rate that may surpass the previous 10,000 years.

The Fourth Law

Technology determines need.

In the old days, the first law of business was, *Find a need and fill it.* In today's rapidly changing, alchemical economy, the opposite is now true: if you want to create wealth, find something to make, and then let it create a demand. The new law is, *Imagine a need, and then create it.*

The fourth law of economic alchemy says that technology doesn't merely help fill a need—technology actually determines what constitutes a "need."

In 1935, at the height of the Great Depression, the brilliant economist John Keynes wrote to President Roosevelt and said, "I can see the day when every American will have a four-bedroom house, a car and indoor plumbing." This, of course, was an absolutely outlandish thing to imagine right in the middle of those bitter years, when millions of people were starving in the street. And of course, it was also great news to FDR.

But Keynes wasn't finished. He went on: "And I can also see the day when the American economy will collapse—because once every American has a four-bedroom house, a car and indoor plumbing, they will have gotten everything they could possibly want and will stop working."

Now we laugh, because we think, "One bathroom?! Who would be satisfied with a house with one bathroom?" Back in the '30s, when most people had outhouses, indoor plumbing sounded pretty amazing. But 50 years after Keynes's letter, every American parent with growing kids knew that at least two bathrooms was a must. And then two cars. And then two TVs. And on it goes.

In the old economics, you had needs: food, shelter and fuel to cook and heat. Because of these basic needs, you had a fixed demand for those things, and because of the "limitations of resources," you had a fixed supply. Supply and demand determined prices.

This has absolutely no application to reality today.

Today, technology invents something that completely changes everyone's way of life, and creates a demand that didn't exist before. Today, "demand" for new products doesn't exist until technology has created the products.

When Henry Ford set out to make affordable automobiles, everyone laughed at him. What does the average man need an automobile for? There were no roads, no gas stations, and besides, everybody lived near the factory or on the farm where they worked, and they worked six or seven days a week. The automobile only made sense as a luxury toy for the rich and leisurely.

And look at what the automobile did. The technology created a demand and transformed everything about our lifestyle. In less than 30 years, our nation was criss-crossed with roads, the automobile transformed everything about our civilization and economy...and of course, everyone *needed* one.

David Sarnoff invented the television the same way. There was no "demand" for television; the invention *created* the demand. Look at computers, cell phones, PDAs, TiVO®. Today, 95 percent of what we spend our money on represents products that didn't even exist a few generations ago.

Just as there is no such thing as a "resource" until we invent it, there is no such thing as a "demand" until our technology creates it. Technology determines need and demand.

The Fifth Law

There is no limit to our economy because there is no limit to demand.

The fifth law of economic alchemy simply says that there is no limit to demand: demand is always going up.

A classical economist will tell you that once you've filled a demand, there's no more room for growth in your industry, as Keynes pointed out in his letter to FDR. But we've seen that this is as far from the reality as can be. You cannot "fill" a demand, because demand is by definition as unlimited as the technology that creates it.

A hundred years ago, the demand for automobiles was zero. We've seen what happened: by the middle of the century, every *family* "needed" a car, and by the end of the century, pretty much every individual *person* needed a car. Once you have a car, is your demand "filled"? Of course not. Not only do you need a new car every few years, but your demand also grows: you don't just want another car, you want a better car—safer, with better mileage, more features, and a nicer interior. If your family owns two Fords, maybe one of you gets a BMW. Then you both get a BMW.

And if you're thinking, "What's wrong with us, aren't we ever satisfied?" know this: it's got nothing to do with being "satisfied." It has to do with the natural direction of human ingenuity, which always devises a new and better way to make new and better things. Can you imagine being "satisfied" with a huge, heavy black and white TV set? Or a modem that ran at 300 baud? Or a car with manual steering and hand-cranked windows?

When you have enough quantity, your demand shifts to a higher quality. And once we have a higher quality, it raises the standard: soon everyone else wants that quality, too, which feeds demand for quantity. It's a never-ending cycle of improvement, refinement and creativity.

The Japanese know this well. In the 1960s, the Japanese flooded the world's markets with cheap merchandise. People under the age of 30 are amazed to hear this, but in the 1960s, "Made in Japan" was a joke; it meant, "really, really cheap stuff." Cheap electronics (transistor radios) and cheap cars (Toyotas and Datsuns): when they broke, you just got another one.

In 1976, when the VCR was introduced, only a few people could afford them because they cost $1,000 and up. Ten years later, Japan had gotten in on the VCR market and the price per unit had dropped from $1,000 to $50. By 1986, there were 110 million U.S. households and 130 million VCRs—that's more than *one per household!*

But during the same time, the Japanese also realized that the Koreans and others would soon make cheap products, too, so they eased themselves out of the "cheap" business and switched to high quality. Toyota turned into Lexus, Datsun turned into Nissan, and the Japanese dominated the high end of the U.S.-invented consumer electronics market. They moved to higher-quality goods because they could see that's where the consumer ends up.

The rhythm of quantity demand and quality demand is a perpetual motion machine of innovation. No matter what anyone tells you, there is always room in the marketplace for growth in one dimension or the other.

A few decades ago, who would have dreamed you could make a serious retail business out of coffee? Back then, a cup of coffee cost a quarter, and coffee was coffee. As a commodity, it wasn't going anywhere, until a Seattle man named Howard Schultz said, "Hey, let's ratchet up the quality!" If I had told you in 1970 that people would pay two or three dollars for a cup of coffee, you'd have laughed at me. But Schultz's company, Starbucks, would have changed your mind. Like the Japanese, Schultz understood the power of quality demand.

The Sixth Law

Your immediate economic potential is defined by your technology gap.

Notice how all these laws work together to define and describe the entire magnificent process of economic alchemy that weaves its threads through the fabric of innovation and wealth creation all around the world.

Laws 1 and 2 describe how technology creates our resources, while Laws 4 and 5 describe how technology creates need and demand. Law 3 describes what it is that creates technology: the exchange of information.

The final law, number 6, describes how all these other laws combine to create specific economic potential. It tells you *where growth is coming from* at any given moment amidst the environment of continuously accelerating change. It tells you where to look to find your greatest immediate economic potential: your technology gap.

People have used the term "technology gap" to describe the disparity between nations, such as between the United States or Western Europe and Third World nations. This is not what I mean when I use the term.

The technology gap I'm talking about is the gap between what technologies people are currently using, and what technologies they could be using, but aren't yet. It is the gap between the way we do something today and the already-developed better way of doing it that we haven't yet utilized.

> *The technology gap is where you will find the greatest potential for growth.*

The technology gap is where you will find the greatest potential for growth. As an entrepreneur, this is where you will find the greatest opportunity. This is where the great majority of the Next Millionaires will come from in the years ahead of us. This is what this book is about.

The first five laws tell us that there is no limit to wealth; the sixth tells us where to find it. It is your treasure map.

Chapter 5

Our Changing World

The overwhelming majority of our social and economic problems today stem from the fact that we have a society built to resist change rather than embrace it.

Human beings resist change automatically. All our biological systems are designed to create a state of constancy within a changing environment: our body temperature, our nerves' sodium/potassium ratios, even our weight, all the systems that comprise the personal ecosystem called "human being" are designed to maintain an unchanging stability despite constantly changing conditions around us.

Because of this, there is a natural human tendency to resist change and to view it as a negative, threatening force.

At the same time, human beings thrive on change. We thrill to innovation and discovery and are delighted with the novel and different. As much as we are comforted by the familiar, we are intrigued by the possibilities of the new.

To survive is to rely on constancy; but to change is to grow. Growth and survival: it is an inherent paradox of human existence.

But today our fundamental relationship to change is itself changing. It has to. In the past, there was security in doing things the same way. Today, the only security that exists lies in embracing change.

Our Alchemical Times

The formula for wealth that you learned in the last chapter, $W = P \times T$, has always been true. Like any valid scientific equation, it is an unchanging, eternal law. However, something about the way it is operating in our world has changed, and drastically so, just in the past century.

Throughout the great majority of history, T has been essentially a constant. Of course, technology has been changing, but only very slowly, over generations.

As a result, during any one individual's lifetime, or during any one king's reign, there was little likelihood of seeing any dramatic change in T. If you were born in the Iron Age, you died in the Iron Age.

Because of this, if you wanted to increase your wealth—whether as an individual citizen, as a king or as an entire society—chances are good the only recourse you could see was to increase P, your physical resources. And again, what this generally meant was go next door, kill your neighbor and take his resources.

That's the history of war, and it's the history of the world—but it's no longer applicable because of the *accelerating rate of technological change.*

It has been only in the last hundred years or so that technology has begun to advance so rapidly. Now, all of a sudden, T is something that can change over the course of a single lifetime—indeed, it can change dramatically.

> *Now, T is something that can change over the course of a single lifetime.*

Let's return to those 30 million farmers in the 1930s whose number dwindled to only three million by the 1980s. What happened to the other 27 million people who got out of farming? They and their children went into other occupations, including manufacturing. Let's take a look at what happened to some of those people.

In the late 1970s, 300,000 of them were employed in the manufacture and maintenance of carburetors. As you already know from the last chapter, we were fast at work improving our automotive technology. In 1980, we introduced the first electronic fuel injector. In 1985, we closed our last carburetor plant. We had fully converted the automobile industry to fuel injectors, doubling fuel economy and halving pollution...and displacing 300,000 workers.

That same year, 1985, there were about 100,000 people in this country employed in the manufacture of vinyl records, which were then the standard medium for musical recordings. By 1990, the last vinyl record plant in the United States shut down. Digital CDs overtook the market in *only five years.* Today, an entire generation doesn't even know what a vinyl record is or what one looks like.

And these changes were *slow,* compared to the speed of change today.

It took 20 years, from 1976 to 1996, to put 135 million VCRs into U.S. households. During 2003 and 2004, the VCR became obsolete, costing another 100,000 people their jobs, when DVD players dropped to $50 or less—a shift that took not 50 years, and not five years, but *less than two years.*

Changes that used to take place in 50 years now happen in a handful of years...or even months. And how we deal with that changing technology explains almost everything.

> *Changes that used to take place in 50 years now happen in a handful of years...or even months.*

That's pretty upsetting if you spent your life in an industry that's suddenly disappeared, but that is exactly what's happening today, and it's going to keep happening at an even faster rate.

Remember the digital CDs that eliminated vinyl records? Just a few years ago, a new technology called MP3 burst onto the scene and captured a huge share of the market. Suddenly kids were downloading MP3s from the Internet instead of buying CDs. Now, look at what's happened here: the move from vinyl to CD had been a shift from one physical medium to another, and it took five years. This time, the music literally leapt off the CDs onto a medium that didn't even involve any physical materials—and it happened over the course of *12 months*.

Because technology changes so fast, it has now become the single most critical component to managing your life economically. Whether for an individual or a nation, economics is about securing your wealth, and the equation for doing that has radically changed.

My French-speaking mother would always say, *"La plus ça change, la plus ça reste le meme chose."* "The more things change, the more they remain the same." True...but the speed of change has been doubling every decade or so, and has now gotten so fast that it has opened up economic opportunity that would have been unimaginable 100, 50 or even 25 years ago.

Where T used to be a constant, today it is the wild card. It is the force at the core of all the laws of economic alchemy, and today it has become that thing which most easily and most rapidly changes. It is your key to creating wealth.

> *T is the force at the core of all the laws of economic alchemy. It is your key to creating wealth.*

The Truth about Unemployment

Today we hear quite a bit about unemployment. While the media focuses its attention on human-interest stories of people displaced from jobs, politicians vie to top each other's promises as to how much more unemployment their policies will eliminate than their competitors' will. But what their promises would really mean (if they could fulfill them) would be to turn back the clock and reverse the natural progression of events.

What they are missing is the connection that *only* unemployment—the kind that results from a change to a newer technology—can create new jobs and grow the size of the economic pie for everyone.

Imagine a self-sufficient desert island community with only ten families, all of whom subsist on fish. Every day, all 10 men go out in their communal boat with their fishing poles, while the ten women stay home to take care of the huts and the children.

Now along comes a missionary who shows the men a new and better technology for fishing: a large net. Using the single net instead of the ten individual poles and lines, now it takes only two fishermen to catch the same number of fish: one to pilot the boat and one to throw the net. The same number of fish, or even more. Amazing!

But now they have a problem. Unemployment in their little island community has just risen from zero to 80 percent!

Notice that the island society as a whole is still just as wealthy as it was before; in fact, since it can preserve the little bit of extra fish it catches, it's growing even slightly wealthier. But eight of the ten fishermen are now out of jobs. How will it feed and clothe these eight unemployed fishermen and their families?

It could pass a law against nets, to prevent unemployment.

Sound ludicrous? That's exactly what many societies do. Or, when a new technology displaces people from jobs, different groups will picket and protest to try to get their politicians to do something to stop the advance.

Or, it could "solve" its "problem" by taxing the two working fishermen and redistributing the earnings to the unemployed fishermen. All this would take would be an income tax rate of, let's see…hmm, 80 percent.

"Ridiculous," you say. "What kind of society would increase the marginal tax rate to 80 percent on the producers of society?"

Us, that's who! During the first half of the twentieth century, that is exactly what we did. This was the world's primary response to short-term unemployment as the implementation of technological advances made certain people far richer than their neighbors. Between 1913 and 1960, the United States and Western Europe instituted highly progressive income taxes, increasing the personal marginal income tax rate to as high as 91 percent (in 1959) on the producers of society.

Let's return to our island community for a moment. What could our island friends do instead? They could help the eight unemployed fishermen develop new jobs that will add to the wealth of the community. One could learn medicine and help raise the level of health for everyone on the island. One could specialize in roofing, and develop stronger and more protective huts. One could specialize in teaching the children, and increase the level of intellectual and creative skills throughout the next generation. And they could both barter their skills with the remaining fishermen as well as with each other—which is exactly why we call it "plying their trade"—and thereby increase both the welfare and the wealth of everyone in the community.

Note that in our island community, none of these jobs or professions—healer, roofer, teacher—existed before. There were only fishermen, and they got by as best they could. It was only after a better technology had increased the productivity of the fishermen 500 percent and caused 80 percent unemployment that these new jobs began to exist.

Just as economic alchemy teaches us that resources don't exist until the human mind creates them, and "demand" doesn't exist until the human mind creates it (through technology), here we can see that *new jobs don't exist until the human mind creates them.*

And what will they do in these jobs? Innovate. Invent. Create. Find better ways of doing each of those tasks.

This is one of the most difficult concepts to understand because of the enormous paradigm shift it represents: *Unemployment is the first and only true sign of economic growth.*

> *Unemployment is the first and only true sign of economic growth.*

Technically speaking, we are talking here about "structural unemployment," which is the economist's term for unemployment caused by technology and represents virtually all the unemployment we see today. The new machine puts people out of work. And while our government fights it, it's the best thing that could possibly happen. Because when the machine puts somebody out of work with the new technology, we as a society still have the output of the work—and now we have more people available to learn new things and innovate in more areas.

I don't mean to be flippant about an enormous social problem. I have tremendous compassion for the people who suffer the results of these displacements. This is why I became an economist—to try to learn how we can alleviate suffering by improving all our economic lot. It's why I teach and write books about this: to help more and more people see how they can take advantage of these bewildering shifts to find new and better ways to earn income and create wealth. And it's why, as you will learn in these pages, I believe the direct selling industry is ideally positioned to help so many people not only earn a living, but also generate massive amounts of wealth.

But we can't confuse compassion with tunnel vision. As a businessperson, you need to understand that unemployment is the first and only true sign of economic growth—and economic growth is the solution, not the problem.

Again, the overwhelming majority of our social and economic problems stem from the fact that we have a society built to fight change rather than deal with it. The answer to the displacement caused by unemployment is not to issue regulations, legislate further unemployment compensation, or try and fight to hang onto the jobs that are disappearing. That is the habitual response of resistance to change.

The solution is to use our resources to retrain and retool our workforce to embrace the new and emerging industries that will be the growth businesses of tomorrow. Indeed, one of the purposes of this book is to train you to do exactly that for yourself.

Because it can be hard to imagine a future that hasn't happened yet, let me give you a dramatic example from the past.

Where Did the Factory Workers Go?

Remember the massive migration from farms to manufacturing? The story doesn't end there.

In the 1960s, manufacturing was the bedrock of America's economic power. Forty percent of Americans worked in manufacturing.

If I had told you in 1960 that by the end of the century, only 20 percent of Americans would work in manufacturing, you would have been shocked. Our manufacturing capacity is today producing more than four times the output it did in 1960—but (as with our huge increase in farm productivity), it does so with less than half the workers.

If I told you this, you'd wonder, "But what will happen to all those other workers? If we go from 40 percent to only 20 percent in manufacturing, with a huge growth in population, we must have huge unemployment!"

I would tell you, "It's not a problem. They'll be working in restaurants. By the end of the century, the restaurant industry will be our single largest employer."

This time, you wouldn't be shocked: you would simply laugh at me. "Impossible!"

"No, listen," I'd say. "Here in 1960, only five percent of the meals in the United States are eaten outside the home. Yet by the end of the century, we will be eating out for 50 percent of our meals."

"Ridiculous," you'd say. And you'd be right: it would have been ridiculous to make that prediction, for four very good reasons.

First, in 1960, only the wealthy could afford to eat out. Back then, if I had said, "Let's go out and eat," my father would have said, "What do you think we are, millionaires?" In 1960, eating out was a luxury.

But even if everyone could have somehow afforded to go out for meals, there wouldn't have been anywhere near enough places for them to eat it. Like a classical economist, you would have counted the restaurants in America and said, "If half the people went out to eat, where would they go? There's no place to put them!"

I would have told you, "Oh no, in the next 40 years, we're going to build 800,000 new restaurants in shopping centers across America."

You would have said, "Where? There's no room for shopping centers!" And I would have told you, "We're going to tear down whole neighborhoods and put up little commercial strips, mainly for restaurants."

This would have seemed even more ridiculous, but let's say you believed me. "There's still a problem here: even if we did do all that, there's a third reason this 'restaurants for the masses' scenario could never happen: people just won't want to go out that much. I mean, how much French food can you eat?"

In 1960, you see, there were very few choices. You could eat fancy, French-style meals, which were expensive and took hours to eat, or cafeteria food. That was pretty much it.

And I would have said, "Oh no, by the twenty-first century there will be restaurants with dozens and dozens of different kinds of ethnic food."

"Yeah? From what countries?"

Now, what could I tell you? Some of these countries didn't even exist yet. How could I tell you about the thousands of Thai restaurants we'd have in the year 2000 when Thailand didn't even exist yet as a country?

Finally, you'd say, "Okay, even if all those things were true, most people don't have that kind of time." Because in 1960, when you went out to eat, it was a several-hour affair. And if I'd told you that over the next few decades, we'd invent an entirely new way of preparing and serving restaurant food that would be defined not by its location, not by its country of origin, not by its price—but by its speed of delivery, and that we'd even call it the "fast food industry," would you have believed it?

Do you see how difficult it can be to comprehend those kinds of transformations that technology creates even in the years just before they happen?

Over the course of only a generation or two, a new industry was born that would have been impossible to conceive of before it happened. And today, these new opportunities don't show up in 40 years, they show up in four years or four months.

Along with unemployment, today we often hear about the economic anguish caused by the emerging global society. China and India are taking over the world, taking away all our manufacturing, high tech and IT jobs. Everything is being moved offshore and outsourced, and America is being left behind.

But this is simply the same phenomenon on a broader scale. Structural unemployment simply means that someone somewhere is doing the same job better, or cheaper, or both; or that consumers have decided they want to move on to a new and better technology.

People are focusing on the wrong issue. "Outsourcing" is not a problem, it's the inevitable, inexorable march of technology; it's natural evolution. The question is where are you going to focus your own entrepreneurial skills?

Remember the sixth law of economic alchemy: the real economic potential lies in the current technology gap. Not in recapturing old jobs and old industries, but in finding those places in our economy where tomorrow's new needs are being forged right now, in the furnace of human ingenuity and creativity.

What value can you add to the economy? In what new and emerging industries can you find a way to apply your capacity to adapt, learn and create new wealth? You, not China or the American corporation, are in control of your own destiny.

Our Economy since 9/11

Every year of this new century, and especially since the events of 9/11, unemployment in this country has increased; or to put it another way, employment as a percent of our population has gone down.

At the same time, our gross domestic product (our output, also referred to as "GDP") has been steadily rising every single quarter-year since September 11, 2001, with only one exception. In the third quarter of 2001, our GDP declined by 0.2 percent, and everyone screamed "Recession!" But the following quarter, the GDP grew again—in fact, by ten times the amount of the decline!

It's not only that our GDP is on the constant rise. More significantly, the ratio of GDP growth relative to interest rates and inflation—which directly translates into consumer lifestyle—is the highest it has ever been in the history of the United States. Our wealth as an individual society has been going up every month consecutively for the last five years.

As proof of this: One of the best true indicators of the real economy that people see every day is home ownership. Today, 69 percent of U.S. households own their own home. This is the highest this key indicator has been in 25 years, and it has increased every year since 2000. If we were in an ailing or faltering economy, how could the number of people owning their own homes be on the increase every month?

At the same time, while our output has risen, total employment has fallen. (Actual employment in the United States today is 140 million, up a little bit from 135 million five years ago, but it's down as a percentage of U.S. population.) There are now eight million people we call unemployed, where there used to be six million—a big increase in the number of people looking actively for work. Yet again, this has occurred even as our output has so dramatically risen.

In other words, even while we are having more and more unemployed fishermen on our little island, we are catching more and more fish!

That means that those people who are employed and the people who own businesses—including entrepreneurs and people with home-based businesses—are wealthier than ever before. How much wealthier? In 2000, the gross domestic product per employed person was $71,000. Today that figure is $84,000. That's huge—a nearly 20 percent increase in wealth or disposable income per employed person. Which translates into a vigorously growing spending power: people with more and more dollars, ready to spend them on more and more new and better things.

All of which is setting the stage for the next wave of economic growth in the second half of this decade.

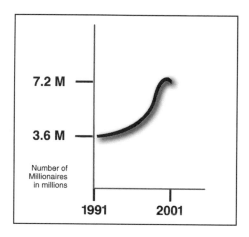

A "Perfect Storm" of Explosive Growth

In the introduction to this book, I said that right now we are looking at the same sort of conditions that occurred in 1990, when we were perched on the threshold of one of the greatest economic boom periods in history. In fact, I said that right now the same conditions apply—only more so.

The fact is everything is poised in a confluence of potential-laden circumstances and trends, pointing to a "perfect storm" of conditions for the most extraordinary explosion of economic growth we have ever seen. Before we go on to look at how you can personally benefit from this amazing historical situation, let's summarize the principles we've learned up to this point that help explain why this time we live in is so rich with economic possibility:

1) THE THEOLOGICAL CONCEPT BEHIND FREE ENTERPRISE

"Create wealth by improving what you have, rather than taking it away from someone else." This was the revelation of Abraham, one of the first lessons humankind learned in the Book of Genesis. This concept of the entrepreneurial development of owned property, when combined with the power of free trade and the free exchange of information, creates limitless possibility for growth and advancement, as well as the foundations for a peaceful, cooperative society.

2) ECONOMIC ALCHEMY

Economic alchemy tells us that we're never running out of anything, because what matters is not the physical resources, it's the technology—in other words, it's how we apply human ingenuity to our environment that literally creates our resources and wealth.

We're never running out of anything, that is, provided we trust one another to keep trading with each other for our specialized output. In fact, the governor of our economic growth, both for nations and for individuals, is not simply how much we produce, but how well we share and distribute what we produce.

Economic alchemy also tells us that we have unlimited growth ahead of us because we're never going to make everything we want. The human mind drives innovation and technology, which drive need and demand, which drive growth. Because the human mind is unlimited, wealth is unlimited.

3) UNEMPLOYMENT CAUSED BY TECHNOLOGICAL CHANGE MEANS GROWTH

Unemployment caused by technology, which is the cause of virtually all unemployment today, is the first and only good sign of economic growth. What we used to call "machines taking jobs" is actually the key indicator of coming great economic growth.

Those who remain employed have more money to spend on growing the economy, and will want new goods and services that didn't exist before. New economic growth occurs when formerly displaced workers become productive again, offering new products and services that expand our lifestyles and create further demand.

4) SPEED OF CHANGE

There is nothing new in all of this except for the speed with which it is happening today and how we deal with it. However, that acceleration in the rate of change has hurtled us into a world where the dynamics of work, innovation and wealth creation have dramatically shifted.

Technology (T) used to be a constant over a human being's lifetime. Today technological change has become something you can control yourself.

Changes that used to take 50 years now occur in just a few years or even months, causing us to deal with the problems of retraining existing employees within single lifetimes as opposed to passively waiting for our descendents to choose other, more productive occupations. At the same time, this rate of change is now opening up new and emerging industries and opportunities with dizzying speed.

Who Wants to Be a Millionaire?

"Who Wants to Be a Millionaire?" "Joe Millionaire." *The Millionaire Next Door. The Automatic Millionaire. The One-Minute Millionaire. Secrets of the Millionaire Mind.* Have you noticed it? In the last few years, every time you turn around, there's another popular TV show or bestselling how-to book about millionaires.

This raft of interest in millionaires is no accident, and it's not just wishful thinking, either. The truth is we're in the middle of a "millionaire population explosion."

> *We're in the middle of a "millionaire population explosion."*

The 1990s were about massive wealth creation. During that decade alone, there were 3.6 million U.S. families who didn't believe the pundits who predicted doom and gloom, and who became millionaires despite the pessimism of their peers. The 2000s are proving to be no different—only more so. Those who start businesses now and get ready for the onrush of this explosion will become the next 3.6 million millionaires in the 2000s.

It took us 215 years, from 1776 to 1991, to create the first 3.6 million millionaires. It took us only ten years (1991–2001) to create another 3.6 million, for a total of 7.2 millionaires. In only a single decade, we doubled the number of million-dollar U.S. households that we had created during the entire history of our nation.

And the millionaire population explosion is still happening.

In the four years from 2001 to 2005, amid the general gloom, malaise and reports of economic stagnation, we continued creating millionaires. How many more? *Another million.* In those few years since the disasters of 9/11, one million

Americans quietly went about their business every day, not wanting to brag about how well things were going for them. They saw unemployment happening all around them, and heard the news telling us how bad everything was, and they didn't want to upset the applecart or seem uncaring. They simply, quietly, became millionaires.

Over the next ten years, we are poised to create an additional ten million millionaires—raising the total number of U.S. millionaires to *more than 18.5 million* by 2016.

The only question is where will those Next Millionaires emerge? And how can *you* be one of them?

> *Over the next ten years, we are poised to create an additional ten million millionaires—raising the total number of U.S. millionaires to more than 18.5 million by 2016.*

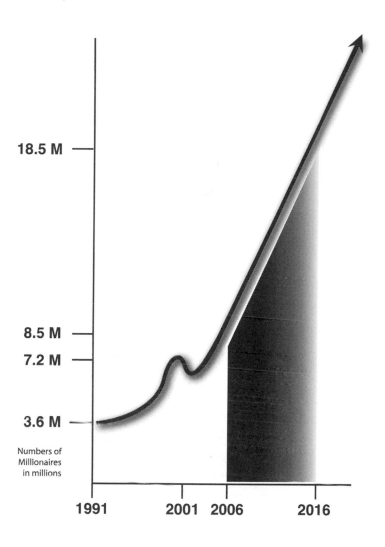

18.5 M

8.5 M
7.2 M

3.6 M

Numbers of
Millionaires
in millions

1991   2001 2006   2016

Chapter 6

Your Personal Economic Alchemy

Your Alchemical Life

It used to be that if your name was Miller, your family made bread. If your name was Smith, your family made steel or worked in a smithy. Your family and your name identified what you would do for the rest of your life. The industrial revolution changed that equation.

At the beginning of the twentieth century, most people were limited to the jobs that existed where they lived. If you grew up near a coal mine, that's where you worked.

Since the advent of the automobile and highway system, that has changed, too. We became a mobile society where people would grow up, leave home in their inexpensive cars and settle hundreds or even thousands of miles away.

But even in our mobile society, most people have been limited in their jobs to their original choices. Once you choose a career, that's your career for life.

No more. All of these established patterns have been swept away by the advance of technology. Today, your work is no longer defined by family, name, location or one-time career choices. It's defined by your skills and how well you keep pace with the dizzying rate of technological advance. Today, the average career lasts seven years; the average job, 20 months.

> *Your work is defined by your skills and how well you keep pace with the dizzying rate of technological advance.*

What Is Your Personal Technology?

W = P x T

The equation W = P x T doesn't apply only to nations. It also applies to you, as an individual entrepreneur. If your own personal wealth equals your personal resources (P) times your technology (T), let's do a quick inventory and find out what those two factors are.

YOUR PERSONAL RESOURCES (P)

In the past, we would have said that for you, P would have been how much land you had, or perhaps how many head of cattle, or how much gold. Today, a more relevant measure of your P is *the people you know.*

> *Today, a more relevant measure of your P is the people you know.*

No matter what your career or what occupations you've had, over the years you have developed relationships with a certain number of people. These are people whose trust you've earned, people who, if you contacted them, would return your call.

The businesses you know from your first-hand experience are also a part of your personal resources. If you have worked in accounting, or in health care, or in sales, or in graphic design, your reservoir of knowledge in that specific industry is a part of your P.

Another part of you P is the amount of time you have. After you deduct that portion of time you devote to basic necessities like sleeping and eating, and the portion of your day you want to spend time with family, friends and other personal pursuits, you have a certain number of hours each day available to devote to work.

So: in your equation, P stands for your relationships, knowledge and available hours.

YOUR PERSONAL TECHNOLOGY (T)

First and foremost, your "personal technology" refers to your *skills.*

Remember how changes in technology during the '70s and '80s allowed us to increase greatly the value we derived from a gallon of oil? And how advances in farming multiplied our productivity per acre by many times? In exactly the same way, you can apply your own personal technology—your skills—to your existing resources (your relationships, knowledge and the available hours in the day) to multiply their productivity. This is why two people can have the same number of hours in the day, or a similar knowledge base, yet achieve very different results.

Your personal technology includes three types of skills.

First are your *basic skills,* which include your ability to read, write, speak, calculate and process information. These are core technological skills that everyone needs, in virtually any type of job or business. If you're limited in those basic skills, now may be the time to improve them.

Next come your *functional skills,* which include whatever specialized skills you have learned to date. If you have worked in nursing, or law enforcement, or counseling, each of these experience sets brings with it a unique skill set. The sum total of these specialized skill sets are what I'm calling your functional skills.

It used to be that the smart strategy to become successful was to learn certain specialized skills, and learn them to a surpassing degree. If you could hone to a razor's edge your typing skills, or your drafting skills, or any number of other specific functional skills, you had a career for life and could command a good salary within that field. No longer. Today, relying on mastery of a specific functional skill is business suicide—because the area in which your skill lies will have completely transformed or disappeared in a matter of years.

Today, your success in business depends largely on the next, third set of skills: your *adapting skills.* What these boil down to is the ability with which you learn new things—which is the single most important skill for any person starting a business today.

> *Success in business depends largely on your adapting skills—the ability with which you learn new things.*

If you come up with a new product or service, what's a competitor going to do? Come up with a similar product for your customer. Who's going to get there faster?

If a field or market you work in goes through a rapid shift or leap in technology, who are people going to turn to so they can understand what's going on and how to work with it? If that person is you, then you are tapping into a huge increase in your T, which means a huge increase in your capacity to create wealth.

To a great degree, you can define your competitive edge and your capacity to create new wealth by how fast and how well you learn something new.

YOUR PERSONAL WEALTH

Now let's put that all together and see how you can apply the lessons of nations and industries to your own personal economic alchemy.

Your W, or your wealth...

equals your P, which consists of...

1. your relationships; the people you know and whose trust you've earned;
2. the businesses you know about from your direct experience; and
3. the amount of time you have available to work;

times your T, which consists of...

1. your basic skills: your ability to read, write, speak, calculate and process information;
2. the functional (specialized) skills you've learned to date; and
3. most important, your ability to adapt to change and learn new skills.

Increasing personal T is what doubled the number of millionaires in the ten years from 1991 to 2001, and then added another million in the last four years. More than any other factor, how you manage your personal T today is what can make you one of the Next Millionaires tomorrow.

So how do you get more T?

> *More than any other factor, how you manage your personal T today is what can make you one of the Next Millionaires tomorrow.*

The Internet: Key to Mastering Your T

In the late 1980s, speaking on the *Larry King Live!* television show, I predicted that one reason we would not have a major recession in the 1990s (contrary to what so many others were predicting) was that we would develop a technology for *instant, real-time communication* between consumers and companies.

People thought what I said was utterly unrealistic—but then something happened. That "something," of course, was the Internet, and it is the single most powerful force driving the growth and transformation of our economy.

You'll remember that throughout history, one of the critical factors in economic expansion has been the building of roads. From the ancient Phoenician shipping trade routes to the massive road-building projects of the Roman Caesars to the great railways system and federal highway network in the United States, networks of roads have always served to move both rapid information exchange and free trade, the two great lubricants of the gears of technological change.

Imagine what the Internet has done—and, more importantly, what it is about to do! The term "information superhighway" is more than just an evocative metaphor. It is itself a new highway system, every bit as much as the Roman viaducts and the U.S. interstates, and has burst open previous limits to trade and communication and multiplied our capacity for economic growth 20-, 50-, 100-fold. Now you can create something in your garage and sell it instantaneously all around the world.

The Internet was first developed in the late '50s and early '60s as a way for the government to maintain communication in the event of nuclear attack. This decentralized network of mainframe computers was called ARPANET, and originally consisted of just four massive computers (located at UCLA, Stanford, University of California at Santa Barbara and the University of Utah). In the 1970s, the original defense department system grew to connect 50,000 universities and research scientists around the globe.

In 1985, a historic decision was made that allowed any university professor to have an Internet account. As a professor at New York University during this time, I first gained access to the Internet.

A decade later, in 1995, an even more historic decision opened the Internet up to everyone. This had the effect of pouring gasoline onto the fire of economic expansion. And that effect is as real for your personal wealth building as it is for societies at large.

If the key to creating more wealth (increasing the W in the equation) is to increase your personal technology (the T), you already know the secret to getting more technology. The third law of economic alchemy tells you how: *technology is determined by the rate of information exchange.*

How you get more technology is by improving your speed of communication.

How you get more technology is by improving your speed of communication.

How well and how fast you know how to communicate through the Internet, to find new products, find new resources, tell your customers about products or services, communicate with the people with whom you work interdependently, research new areas, learn new knowledge and new skills—how well and fast you know how to do all that and more—is going to determine your capacity to build wealth in the twenty-first century.

No matter what your particular area or in what field you apply your entrepreneurial energies, the Internet is your most important technology for turning your existing resources into those of a millionaire.

> *The Internet is your most important technology for turning your existing resources into those of a millionaire.*

Mastering Your Technology Gap

Let's say you drive to work every day following a certain route. It's the route you take because it's the route everyone takes. Then one day, there's a bad accident at a major intersection. Traffic's stopped for blocks. What can you do?

Grumbling, you turn your car around, head back a few blocks, then pick your way through a few side streets and find a different way to work. And lo and behold: although it's more mileage and uses all these back streets, your new route actually gets you to work faster!

The "detour" that turned out to be a new and better way of getting there had been available for months. You just never thought to try it, until an accident forced you to. And that's exactly the problem with most businesses in America today, both huge companies and individual entrepreneurs: we wait until the accident to go out and find the new and better way.

Because people resist change, we allow the technology gap to widen and widen, without exploring it. We don't change suppliers when things are working okay as they are. We don't try new software, new tools, new technologies. We say, "If it ain't broke, don't fix it"—and we end up losing out to those who took the initiative to find new and better ways *before* the accident, those who are actively exploring their technology gap and who never wait for the accident to happen. The motto of the successful businessperson today is, "If it ain't broken yet, good— now go find a better one!"

And herein lies the key to success. Recall what the sixth and final law of economic alchemy tells us: your immediate economic potential is defined by your technology gap. Here's what this means: how well you explore that area of "what you don't know about yet," and how regularly and rigorously you explore it, how much you discipline your mind to step out of its routines and look into new ways of doing things that you haven't yet adopted, is what will determine your economic potential.

> *How much you discipline your mind to step out of its routines and look into new ways of doing things that you haven't yet adopted is what will determine your economic potential.*

Now you know that there is no limit to resources, no limit to technology, no limit to demand and no limit to wealth. Aren't there any limits on anything?!

Yes. In fact, there is one thing that is limited, and this is perhaps your most precious resource, for it can never be replaced, no matter how wealthy, clever or powerful you are: your time.

You cannot grow more hours in the day. However, you can make better use of those hours, just as American farmers learned to make better use of the same number of acres. And there is nothing more important in leveraging your time than the Internet—from scheduling and e-mail to videoconferencing and making presentations.

> *You cannot grow more hours in the day. However, you can make better use of those hours.*

Just as the computer is more than simply a glorified typewriter (which is exactly how most people used it at first), the Internet is far more than simply a glorified phone directory (which is how many are still using it today). It is an instantaneous global communication system. Your ability to use it to leverage your time is the key to your success.

Chapter 7

Go Where the Growth Is

Remember what adults asked you when you were a child? "What do you want to be when you grow up?" And what did they ask you in school? "What do you want to major in? What are you going to be?"

The idea was that you were going to "be" one thing, and "be" that for the rest of your life. How many people do you know who have done the same thing since they graduated from school? Anyone?

You can no longer just pick a job and keep it for the rest of your life. Remember what happened to 27 million farmers over 50 years: this is now happening everywhere in our economy on a scale of just a few years, and sometimes, just months!

The question is not, will you find yourself working in a new industry? The question is, which one?

> *You can no longer just pick a job and keep it for the rest of your life.*

New and Emerging Industries

The greatest fortunes to be made in the years ahead will not be made in what people were doing five, 10 or 15 years ago. They will be made in industries that barely even exist today.

One of the great challenges of innovation is that by definition, it's practically impossible to predict what it will be before it happens. And the last place to look is at existing demand.

The fourth law of economic alchemy tells us that demand and need don't drive technology: it's the other way around. Technology creates a new product, and that product's existence creates the need. There was no need for the Sony Walkman®, but once the device existed, people discovered they could listen to music while they jogged—and suddenly everyone *needed* one!

If you go into an existing industry, as an entrepreneur, you're always going to be just working harder. You're going to put in a lot more hours and work a lot harder to try to beat the competitor, and have smaller chances of great success.

But if you go into a new or emerging industry, working smarter instead of simply harder, you can be the one distributing the new product that will be in demand because it will improve people's lives. The only trick is you have to be alert to see what is new and emerging—because once everyone else has noticed, it will no longer be new and emerging!

We've already talked a good deal about the automobile, but it's worth pointing to again here: the personal car is a great example of a "new and emerging industry" that seemed absolutely ludicrous to most people at first, yet it grew to become one of the greatest industrial, technological and sociological forces of the twentieth century. From entertainment to industry, dating to demographics, there was not an aspect of human life that was not radically transformed in the last century by the automobile. Yet when Henry Ford set out to build an "affordable automobile," it looked like sheer lunacy.

In the 1970s, the very idea of a "personal computer" was hilarious. How could a computer be personal? It was the ultimate oxymoron! For one thing, it cost millions of dollars. For another thing, it filled an entire room. And besides...what the heck would you *do* with it?

Twenty years ago, when Bill Gates and Michael Dell set out to create their own businesses (respectively, Microsoft and Dell Computers), they were both heading in a direction as unlikely as Henry Ford was in the 1920s: they were working in an industry that didn't yet exist. A decade later, they had become two of the richest men in the world

The first IBM personal computer (PC) came out in 1981. By 1990, PC sales exceeded automobile sales, and by the turn of the century, personal computers had become a trillion-dollar industry. *One trillion!*

The automobile and the PC are two excellent examples of new and emerging industries of the past. In this chapter and the next, we'll look at three examples of new and emerging industries that are just now getting underway: wellness, the Internet, and the type of distribution I call "intellectual distribution," best represented by the distribution channel known as *direct selling* (also known variously as *network marketing, multilevel marketing* or *party-plan marketing*).

The Wellness Business

What we call the "health care" business is not really the health business but the *sickness* business. Our medical industry today has very little, if anything, to do with health. The $1.4 trillion we spend on medical care, which represents one-seventh of the U.S. economy, is concerned with treating the symptoms of illness. It has very little to do with preventing illnesses or with making people feel stronger or healthier.

Today, however, there's a brand new industry that has nothing to do with sickness but is all about creating wellness. Wellness doesn't treat people who are sick or address illness. Wellness is for people who are already well and who want to stay well, slow down the aging process, or keep from becoming customers of the sickness business.

Here is how I define wellness:

> *Wellness is money you spend to make you feel healthier, even when you're not "sick" by any standard medical terms.*

Dollars spent in the wellness industry are spent to make you stronger, to make you see better, to make you hear better, to fight what we might call the symptoms of aging.

Ten or 15 years ago, it would have been tough to go into the wellness industry. Why not? Because there was no wellness industry. What happened?

Well, the phenomenon of aging has obviously been around for as long as life itself, so it wasn't as if there was a sudden spontaneous "need" for a wellness industry. The wellness business showed up in the last decade due to new technology.

Who would have imagined that we "needed" to create a product to address sexual performance for 70-year-olds? Geriatric impotency is not exactly a medical problem that society was worrying about. When it hit the market in 1998, the whole world started making Viagra® jokes—but notice, we all accepted that the product works. Not only that: it became an instant $10 billion business.

Viagra for sexual performance, Rogaine® for hair growth, cosmetic dentistry and elective plastic surgery, antioxidants and other supernutritionals…all these new products and more enhance quality of life and slow down the aging process, and they all are the result of recent advances in technology.

To the $70 billion in vitamins and food supplements, you can add $24 billion in fitness club memberships. A generation ago, whoever heard of joining a fitness club? In 1975, jogging was regarded as a "craze," a fringe thing, like the hula hoop, that would go away quietly if we just gave it time. The idea that an entire nation would consider running as a normal, everyday activity would have been seen as lunacy.

To this $94 billion, you also need to add another $12 billion paid to personal trainers. Personal trainers?! Twenty years ago, nobody would have believed it. A top-paid athlete, sure, but everyday people, actually paying someone to show them how to step on and step off a machine, just to stay fit? Who would pay for such a thing? We would: $12 billion worth.

When you add up all the different facets and aspects of wellness, you find that it is already a $300 billion business. And this is only the beginning, because most people don't even know these products exist, or don't think they are applicable to them. As the rest of the population begins to learn about wellness, this sector will explode. At the rate it's going, I project that, just as the PC industry did ten years ago, by the end of this decade, the wellness industry will exceed $1 trillion.

> *By the end of this decade, the wellness industry will exceed $1 trillion.*

The Internet: It's Barely Gotten Started!

Nobody knew what the Internet was in 1990; consumers weren't even allowed to get their own accounts and private e-mail addresses until 1995. Yet by the turn of the century five years later, many new millionaires in this country were being created by or over the Internet.

More than any other factor, the Internet is driving this millionaire population explosion—and I'm not speaking only of those entrepreneurs who are in an obviously Internet-related business, such as amazon.com® or eBay®. Just as the written word created the burst of creativity we call "civilization" and the printed word created that explosion of growth we call "industrialization," the globally-everywhere-instantaneous "real-time word" communication that the Internet provides is creating an entirely new age that we barely even have a name for yet; if we did, we might call it "informationalization."

Do you understand why this is so? It's the third law of economic alchemy: the growth of new technology is determined by the rate of information exchange. The birth of the Internet has so dramatically accelerated the exchange of information that it is creating the greatest new burst of creativity and wealth creation we've seen since the printing press.

We've seen that the Internet—and specifically, your ability to use it to leverage your time and increase your learning—is one of the most important tools you need to create wealth. Even in an asset-based industry such as real estate, today it is what you do with your property versus how much property you own that will determine your success. And the Internet is the key to this.

Because of the "Internet bubble," those few years in the late 1990s when investors poured billions of dollars into sometimes highly speculative Internet-based companies irrespective of their showing any kind of profits or even earnings, many people now have a pessimistic or fatalistic view about the future of the Internet. "Oh, the Internet opportunities...they've come and gone, and it wasn't all it was cracked up to be."

Nothing could be further from the truth! The fact is the Internet is a new and emerging growth super-industry that has barely gotten started. It is about to jump off our desktops and PC screens, onto our cell phones and into every aspect of our lives.

> *The Internet is a new and emerging growth super-industry that has barely gotten started.*

The Internet Goes Local

As important as the global economy is, here is a sobering economic fact: the average consumer spends the majority of his or her consumer dollars within ten miles of home!

What would it be like if you could hop onto the Internet and find out, among all the auto repair shops within a 20-minute drive, which ones have the part you need in stock?

Imagine if you could scroll a screen on your cell phone and find the best day-care center in your area, with the best customer satisfaction ratings—and one that lets you tie into its webcam so that at any point in the day, you can check in and see how your child's doing?

Before long, when you want to go to a restaurant, the first thing you'll do is check on your cell phone screen to see which restaurants have seats available. If they have seats they think they're not going to fill, they'll give you a discount on them if you show up immediately. They did it on airplanes; they'll do it with restaurants.

Now, this may seem like nothing more dramatic than a mild improvement in convenience; but think about this: roughly three-quarters of the food grown on our planet each year ends up in the trash instead of in people's mouths. How much food does that restaurant throw away? And what could everywhere-real-time information do to change that figure, globally?

By the end of this decade, when you're waiting at a bus stop shelter, you'll see a little meter telling you how many minutes till the bus will arrive, so you'll know if you have time to run and get coffee. More importantly, the bus driver will know who's waiting at each shelter, and will know which stations to stop at to pick up. If there's nobody there, he or she won't even need to stop.

Again, a slight improvement in convenience, right? But think for a moment: can you imagine how much fuel is wasted making stops where there are no passengers? Or idling at red lights when there is no traffic coming the other way?

With virtually every resource we consume—fuel, food, air, water, you name it—the pressing issue is not limits to supply, it's waste versus smarter usage. As we start communicating and integrating information both globally and locally, applications like this will create an enormous savings of time, energy, fuel and more.

The Internet and Health Care

Another area where the Internet will have enormous impact is health care.

One major reason that our health care system today is in such terrible shape (and remember, we're talking about one-seventh of our economy here) is that it delivers very little in consumer choice. In most cases, it sells the consumer a product that may or may not be the best service or prescription for that consumer's ailment.

> *One major reason that our health care system today is in such terrible shape is that it delivers very little in consumer choice.*

For example, doctors prescribe what they've been given incentives in their area to prescribe. Every year, about one-quarter of the prescriptions written in the United States go unfilled because they cost too much. The Internet will bring the same level of consumer choice to health care that it has brought to so many other areas of the retail world.

The Internet will soon allow a patient to sign on, put in his or her specific ailment, see the drug he or she is taking—and also see 20 different drugs other people are taking for the same condition. He or she will then be able to talk to other people about those drugs, print a report on a specific drug, and bring all that information in to the doctor and have a discussion about it right then and there, to decide whether or not he or she should go on this particular drug.

There is no consumer anywhere in the world more hungry for information than a consumer with a disease—or with a loved one with a disease. The Internet will give health care consumers a choice and it will deliver all that information to them at their fingertips.

The Empowered Consumer and the Empowered Entrepreneur

One of the most transforming effects of the Internet has been the empowerment of the consumer. In the past, salespeople and brokers could usually lead their customers toward the choices they wanted them to buy. Consumers simply didn't know any better, and relied upon these specialists to help them make their buying decisions.

> *One of the most transforming effects of the Internet has been the empowerment of the consumer.*

Not any more. In every field, from health insurance to electronics, from education to stock trading to home buying, more than 50 percent of American consumers are already going onto the Internet to learn everything there is to know about the options available to them. And they can reach out and get opinions and experiences from 50 or 100 other consumers who've recently made similar choices.

Consumers make choices based on knowledge they gain themselves, not on the advice or filtered knowledge of the brokers. And this is forcing quality ever upward, even as it drives prices further downward. It is accelerating the process of economic alchemy.

Even as it empowers consumers, the Internet puts that same power to learn into the hands of the individual entrepreneur, hugely accelerating the process of innovation and wealth creation. Remember, in the new economy, the most important skill is the capacity to learn new things.

What you're going to find is that when it comes to a new business that you're a little confused about, whether it's a wellness business or a technology business or a direct selling business or anything else, you're going to have the best teachers, trainers and tools available to teach you and your customers if you know how to use the Internet.

Chapter 8

Intellectual Distribution: The New Game in Town

It's interesting to look back through history and ask, where do millionaires come from? It's even more interesting if that historical look back can also give us what we need to know to look in the years just ahead and see where the Next Millionaires are coming from. And that's exactly what a clear historical view tells us.

For thousands of years, economic opportunity has largely been in the hands of those who controlled physical resources. The way to become a millionaire was to get your hands on control of large amounts of land, steel, grain, cattle or other critical physical economic staples, either by owning them outright or by controlling the transportation of those resources, as did the great shipping and railway magnates.

This was the era of the "resource millionaires."

Of course, there are still resource millionaires (and billionaires) today, but that's no longer where the real opportunity lies.

For the past two centuries, great opportunity opened for the pioneers, innovators and masters of manufacturing. Especially in the decades after World War II, huge numbers of people became millionaires by finding cheaper ways of making things, often by shipping production overseas and using new materials like plastics. The economy boomed, and people got rich by making better and better things.

This was the era of the "manufacturing millionaires."

But then something happened. During the '60s, '70s and '80s, these bright young entrepreneurs so improved the technology of manufacturing, converting all the expensive raw materials and labor into plastics and flexible automated manufacturing processes, that they completely restructured the economics of retail and created a whole new area of opportunity.

The Rise of the Distribution Millionaires

Back in the 1950s or 1960s, when you went into a department store and bought an item, about 50 percent of the retail price represented manufacturing costs; the other 50 percent represented distribution costs.

Take a typical $300 item, say, a television, camera or dress. In the '50s and '60s, manufacturing costs would account for about half that cost, or $150. The other $150 would represent costs of distribution, from manufacturer to wholesaler to retailer. Distribution also included marketing, advertising and point-of-purchase merchandising. In other words, it cost $150 to make the item, and another $150 to do everything necessary to take it from the manufacturer's plant to the consumer's hands.

But those amazing advances in technology drove those manufacturing costs down so far and so fast that by the 1990s, the cost of manufacturing represented only about 20 percent of the typical retail item's price, with the other 80 percent being distribution costs!

And by the way, just because the cost of distribution had gone from 50 percent to 80 percent of the price tag doesn't mean actual distribution costs went up. They actually went *down,* just not nearly as far down as manufacturing. If you bought that same item that cost $300 in 1960, with comparable quality and features, in 1990 it would cost only $100. The $150 distribution cost in 1960 had been cut roughly in half, to $80—but the 1960 manufacturing cost of $150 had dropped *ten times,* to only $15.

By the '90s, the same item still sold for $300, but it was a far superior product with a great many more features—yet its manufacturing cost had *fallen* from $150 to $15! Now, 80 to 85 percent of the product's costs was in distribution; only 15 to 20 percent was in manufacturing.

In other words, by 1990, the greatest opportunities for wealth were no longer in manufacturing but in distribution. This is why the richest people in the world in 1990 were people who found better ways of distributing things versus better ways of making things.

Back in 1961, Sam Walton started a company that was committed to never making its own brand—it would sell only other name-brand goods. Wal-Mart pioneered the use of technology to control inventory and lower costs, and by 1990, not only was Wal-Mart the largest retailer in the world, Sam Walton was also the richest person in the world—a man who made his living distributing things that other people made.

In 1990, Fred Smith was the most successful airline entrepreneur of the day. Back in 1976, he had started an airline with its own fleet of planes and pilots— yet it didn't fly people! Its only purpose was to move packages. Federal Express linked the country and much of the world with rapid, guaranteed delivery service distribution—an unheard-of idea in 1976.

Ross Perot built a $3.5 billion dollar computer company, Electronic Data Systems (EDS) that made neither software nor hardware. What did EDS do? It distributed other people's hardware and software. By 1990, Ross Perot was one of the wealthiest people in the world.

This was the era of the "distribution millionaires."

Just as the edge of opportunity had shifted from resources to manufacturing, now it shifted again, from manufacturing to distribution.

But that's the past—not the future.

The Next Shift

So, where will the Next Millionaires come from?

The opportunity of the mass merchandisers—the Wal-Marts, Targets and Home Depots—has already come and gone, and it has given birth to a new and even greater opportunity.

In 1999, this new opportunity was dramatically underscored when a businessperson made *Time* magazine's "Man of the Year." This is especially meaningful because it's quite rare for a businessperson to earn that distinction. Who was it? Jeff Bezos, who revolutionized the distribution of books with amazon.com.

Jeff Bezos is one of the new generation of entrepreneurs. Clearly, he is in the distribution business. But look closer. You don't sign on to amazon.com just to physically get the book; you sign on to *learn about* the book. You read the various reviews, look at other books in the category, you may even log on to find out if there even *is* a book on the particular topic you want. And amazon.com doesn't actually distribute the book to your door; once you've decided what you want and paid for it, they let UPS or FedEx do that.

Entrepreneurs like amazon.com founder Jeff Bezos (age 41, net worth $4.3 billion) and eBay founder Pierre Omidyar (age 38, net worth $8.5 billion) are poised to surpass the physical distribution billionaires of yesterday. They are not cast from the same mold as Wal-Mart and Costco. They are a new breed, and they do something distinctly different from the warehouse giants.

The Two Arms of Distribution

For 100 years, prior to the emergence of Wal-Mart, Target and Costco, retailing in the United States was dominated by department stores like Macy's, Filene's and Marshall Fields. These distribution giants fulfilled the two critical functions of distribution: education and delivery. They told consumers about what products and services were available, and they also put those products and services into their hands. This is a time-honored combination of functions that goes back to merchants and peddlers through the centuries.

But as the entrepreneurs of the last few decades pioneered extraordinary new distribution technologies, a large and growing chasm split these two functions apart. Again, these two functions are:

EDUCATION: Teaching consumers about products and services that will improve their lives, typically items that they either don't know exist or don't know are now affordable.

DELIVERY: Physically putting into the consumers' hands the products and services they already know they want.

Delivery, or physical distribution, is where Wal-Mart, Target, Costco and all the distribution giants place their focus. You know exactly what you want when you walk into a Wal-Mart: you go in, pick it up and get out of the store. In the interests of price, convenience and speed, the mass merchants left out a critical aspect of the buying transaction. They stripped away the *intellectual distribution* part of the equation. Wal-Mart doesn't take the time to teach anyone about new products or services. They sell their customers exactly, and only, what the customers already knew they wanted before they walked into the store.

When I wrote *Unlimited Wealth* in 1990, I predicted this physical distribution boom that would dominate the 1990s. But now the bulk of that boom has come and gone; the fortunes to be made there are mostly already made. The fortunes to be made in the years ahead will be predominately not in *delivery* but in *education*—not in *physical distribution,* but in *intellectual distribution:* educating consumers about products and services that will improve their lives...but that they *didn't yet know existed.*

This is the great opportunity of the huge and growing technology gap. It is the #1 business opportunity for those who want to create new wealth. And it is where a great number of the Next Millionaires are coming from.

> *The #1 business opportunity for those who want to create new wealth is educating consumers about products and services that will improve their lives.*

Stepping into the Technology Gap

Why is *intellectual distribution*—educating consumers about products and services they don't yet know about—where so many of the Next Millionaires will come from? Why is it such a huge opportunity? Because that is precisely where the biggest bottleneck is today.

No matter what the industry, the pace of technological change has so rapidly accelerated that today, by the time you learn about a product and are ready to buy it, there's already a better one out there somewhere. Why aren't you and all the other consumers buying this newer model? Because you don't know about it yet. This is what manufacturers call "backlog."

Twenty-five years ago, it was a shock when a clerk in a store couldn't answer your questions. Today, it's normal. Nobody expects the clerk to know much about the product: now that's the consumer's job. There are a few specialty retailers left, where clerks fulfill that traditional role of educating the customer. But in general, the retailers have completely abandoned the traditional function of teaching people about products. Instead, they have focused on the function of efficiently and inexpensively delivering the product.

Go into a showroom and talk to a car salesperson: does that salesperson actually own the car you're talking about? Not likely. Go into an electronics outlet: how often will you meet a salesperson who actually owns the particular product you're considering—or who can even afford to? Seldom. These people are in the business of showing you where to find it on the shelf; they're not there to teach you what it is.

So, where do we learn today? Nowhere. That's the problem—and that's the opportunity. Because *that's the technology gap.*

Remember the sixth and final law of economic alchemy? "Your immediate economic potential is defined by the technology gap." This is it. Today, because technology is advancing so rapidly and making so many new products that can dramatically improve the quality of people's lives, the gap between what people are using and *what they could be using if they only knew about it* is huge and growing huger even as you read these words.

And if you are the one who tells them about that technology, you stand to make a fortune.

> *Today, because technology is advancing so rapidly and making so many new products that can dramatically improve the quality of people's lives, if you are the one who tells them about that technology, you stand to make a fortune.*

Chapter 9

The Age of the Entrepreneur

The traditional wisdom in the second half of the twentieth century was this: go to school, get a good education and go to work for a good company. The idea of "going into business for yourself" was most often regarded as risky. Admirable, perhaps, but risky...and maybe a little crazy.

Today, it's completely the other way around.

Today, it's risky to work for a corporation!

Today, it's far *more* sensible to go to work for yourself.

We're in the midst of a boom in home-based businesses, and it shows no sign of slowing. More than one out of every eight U.S. households contains a home-based business. In 2000, more than 50 percent of all small firms were home-based businesses, and they generated about ten percent of the nation's entire economic receipts.

> *We're in the midst of a boom in home-based businesses, and it shows no sign of slowing.*

In this chapter, we'll look at some of the major reasons why the entrepreneur and home based businessperson have the edge today. New legislation and new technology have caught up with a shift in values: people want to stay home, and now they can. In fact, now people who work from home have the edge!

The Technological Edge

When I graduated from Wharton in 1976, I went to work at Citibank, but it wasn't because I was interested in banking. I wanted access to the best technology, and I knew that Citibank had the biggest and best computers available.

Back then, that was the only way to have access to the best technology. Computers were expensive mainframes owned and internally managed exclusively by large businesses, which gave these major corporations an enormous economic advantage. With the biggest and best computers, we decimated our competition at other banks that didn't have the computers and were still using a paper-based banking system.

Today, the opposite is the case. Today, you are more likely to find the hottest and best new technology sitting on the desk of the individual entrepreneur sitting in his home office! The big companies just can't innovate fast enough.

Today, five of the ten highest-valued companies in the U.S. stock market (Cisco, Microsoft, Intel, Oracle and Vodaphone) are companies that didn't exist 20 years ago, yet today their combined net worth exceeds $1 trillion. What do they have in common? They are all *third-party suppliers of affordable technologies to individual users.*

These leading-edge companies make tools that help the homebuilder build a home faster; tools that help home-based businesspeople communicate, run their businesses and distribute their products better. Remember, these are tools geared towards the individual, not toward some big mainframe computer. Go check out the computer at a typical big corporation today: what you'll generally find is computers that are three, four, five, eight years old.

Here is the edge the individual entrepreneur has over the large corporation: the entrepreneur has little or no bottleneck. The technology gap in a corporation is huge. Technology is changing more rapidly than ever, and in a large organization, it is a monumental challenge to figure out how to bring in and integrate an entirely new generation of technology.

In the '70s and '80s, the rule was, the bigger the company, the newer and better the technology.

Today the rule is, the bigger the company, the older and more out-of-date the technology!

Today, technology is geared toward a fast-moving, highly adaptable business climate based on the personal, one-on-one transaction. As Dell Computers proved dramatically, it's no longer economical to make one model and force everyone to use it. Now, it's more economical to produce whatever customized model that individual customer wants!

Tools and technology for the individual entrepreneur are now the best place to be: the best and brightest companies of the world realize that the growth of

America is going to be in individual entrepreneurs and one-person or two-person businesses. The corporation has been decentralizing and dismantling itself, giving way to an environment of independent contractors, and the tool providers know it. They want to make the tools for the biggest market. And that's the individual entrepreneur.

Where are the greatest opportunities today? Even for people starting out right out of school, the best opportunities are not to go work for big companies (unless it's the companies that make tools for individuals), but to go into business for themselves as entrepreneurs.

> *The greatest opportunities today are to go into business for yourself as an entrepreneur.*

Corporations Can't Compete

So much has changed since the days when I entered the work force 30 years ago. Back then, our employers told us, "We'll always be around, and we'll always take care of you. If you're loyal to us, we'll give you wonderful medical benefits and great retirement packages."

Year by year, we've seen all these big-company promises disappear into thin air. It's not that they're evil people, or that they don't want to keep offering the ideal work environment. It's just that they can't: they are going the way of the dinosaurs.

To understand why it's now lumbering off into extinction, let's take a quick look at how and why the huge corporation came to exist in the first place.

In 1931, an idealistic 21-year-old British college student named Ronald Coase won a scholarship to come study in the United States. A student of economics, he was quite excited to come to "the Land of the Entrepreneur," the home of Horatio Alger, Henry Ford and Andrew Carnegie, where anyone could start from scratch and build a great company.

When he arrived, he found a land in the midst of a great depression, where everyone wanted a job with a company. "Why," he wondered, "in such a great free-market economy, in this land of opportunity, would workers voluntarily submit to working for someone else, when they could go into business for themselves and sell their skills directly to customers in the marketplace?" In other words, why do these big companies even exist, instead of millions and millions of self-employed entrepreneurs?

As Coase studied this question in detail, he found that big companies exist-ed because it was a far more efficient way of doing business. The "transaction costs" of individuals doing business together who weren't under one roof were so high—with transportation costs, telephone expenses, correspondence costs, postal delays, accounting and bookkeeping costs, and so on—that the expense would exceed their economic output. (All these transactions were quite labor-intensive; in these days of manual bookkeeping, for example, it often took as much as one accountant for every three workers simply to keep track of billing and payment and proper categorization of expenses.)

Because of these enormous transaction costs, Coase predicted the rise of gigantic vertical corporations. His paper, entitled "The Nature of the Firm," became the standard work on the subject. Coase went on to become a professor at the University of Chicago; 60 years later, in 1991, he won the Nobel Prize in Economics for his famous paper.

But things have changed. Remember expensive long-distance telephone? Manual double entry bookkeeping? Expensive overnight delivery? They're all relics of the past. Today, thanks to advances in technology, all of these transaction costs have suddenly fallen to near zero.

In fact, I recently re-visited Professor Coase's original equations using today's data, and discovered that they now point to exactly the opposite conclusion: it is now so much more efficient to work in very small units that many of our large organizations should no longer even exist. And that is exactly what we see hap-pening: today's most important and most viable "corporations" are those that are going *virtual*. Much of the unemployment we are experiencing today actually represents the permanent dismantling of many of our large corporations as they are out-competed by smaller companies, independent contractors and other fast-adapting, quick-moving entrepreneurs.

Individuals have debated leaving their jobs and becoming entrepreneurs since the first large employers emerged in the nineteenth century. In the past, this debate has always focused on the opportunity and risk of going out on one's own. Today, the real risk is staying with a large organization, because your job will probably be permanently dismantled within a few years.

> *Today, the real risk is staying with a large organization, because your job will probably be permanently dismantled within a few years.*

The Benefits

If you were a millionaire 20 years ago, chances are good the way you made your money was by building a business and *then selling it*. Why? Because, ordinary (vs. capital gains) income taxes were 70 and 80 percent, and the only people who could have pension funds, 401(k) and deferred savings were people who worked for big companies. What's more, the only people who could get healthcare coverage were people who worked for a big company.

No longer.

Some critical changes have happened recently in U.S. tax laws (some of which I'm proud to say I had something to do with). These changes now make it possible for you to accumulate millions of dollars with ordinary cash flow from a home-based business, in ways that were not available to you before—*if* you know how to take advantage of them. Congress has finally created a level playing field for individual entrepreneurs by creating tax laws that make it possible for entrepreneurs to enjoy the same benefits of tax-free or tax-deferred savings as employees of corporations.

> *Congress has finally created a level playing field for individual entrepreneurs by creating tax laws that make it possible for entrepreneurs to enjoy the same benefits of tax-free or tax-deferred savings as employees of corporations.*

One reason many people work for large organizations is for the medical and retirement benefits. From 1944 until 2005, employees of large companies enjoyed a 2-to-1 or better tax advantage over individuals when it came to paying for benefits. This was because: (1) employees who get free or low-cost health benefits don't have to pay income taxes on them; (2) their employers are allowed a 100-percent tax deduction for health benefits they provide; and (3) the employees can defer paying taxes on contributions their employers make to their retirement plans.

But now, individual entrepreneurs can actually get better health and retirement benefits than employees of large companies. The best health insurance available today for most families is an individual, rather than group, policy, because the premiums on an individual policy cannot generally be raised because of illness. And new Health Savings Accounts (HSAs) give individuals the same tax advantages as corporate employees.

> *Now, individual entrepreneurs can actually get better health and retirement benefits than employees of large companies.*

Since 2003, there have been individual health insurance policies that are both affordable and tax-deductible for self-employed people. Employees, on the other hand, typically are stuck with group plans for which the premiums are raised each year based on the prior year's claims. Such group plans are a ticking time bomb as the group ages.

Most people think of Individual Retirement Accounts (IRAs) as small insignificant retirement accounts. However, beginning 2005, a working couple can contribute $8,000 annually to an IRA, rising to $10,000 in 2008. IRAs not only allow all the benefits of a traditional corporate retirement plan, they also allow tax-free early withdrawals at any age for life events such as a first-time home purchase or the payment of health insurance premiums while unemployed.

If you have your own business, the retirement savings options are even better! With a self-employed retirement account such as a SEP IRA or a One-Person 401(k)/Profit Sharing Plan, you can put away up to $41,000 per year—pretax—and become a millionaire in 15 years of working for yourself as an entrepreneur. You couldn't do that before without working for a big company.

Why did Congress change these laws and create such wonderful incentives? They had to. Today more than 50 percent of Americans work either for themselves or for a small business.

> *Today more than 50 percent of Americans work either for themselves or for a small business.*

The Lifestyle

In the new economy, the sheer quantity of compensation is no longer enough. More and more, we have come to realize we also want a certain quality of compensation, too. We don't simply want money, we want *lifestyle.*

It doesn't matter how much money you earn if you never get to see your spouse or children. It doesn't matter how many physical possessions you have if you never get to play with them. And it doesn't matter how great a personal economy you create if you don't have the health to enjoy it.

The concept of "quality of life," which we take for granted today, is actually a fairly recent invention, just as is "customer service," and for exactly the same reason: the advance of technology. Our economy and living standards have grown to the point where we not only expect to make a living (or complete a transaction), but we also expect to have the *best possible experience* living that life (or making the transaction). "Quality of life" is the same concept as "good customer service" extended for our entire life span!

This harkens back to the fourth and fifth laws of economic alchemy: technology determines demand, and demand is without limit. Now we demand a quality of life that gives us not only survival, but also a depth of meaning and fulfillment. And here again, a corporate job simply can't compete with self-employment.

Make no mistake about it: when you start your own business, you're going to put in the same hours as you did working for the corporation, if not more. But you get to control *which* hours.

> *When you start your own business, you're going to put in the same hours as you did working for the corporation, if not more. But you get to control which hours.*

I work at home from a wireless laptop—in fact, I have wireless laptop and wireless phone access in every room of the house, so I'm free to go anywhere throughout my home and be "at work" any time I want. I can spend an hour with my kids at breakfast if that's important to me. I can put my hours in after my kids are all asleep. I decide which hours I'm going to put in, rather than someone else arbitrarily deciding for me.

We often talk today about the challenge of keeping a balance between our work and our families. Picture it like a seesaw, with work on one end and family on the other. When you're constantly playing these priorities against each other, your life swings and swings until eventually the whole thing breaks, whether that means losing the job, losing the family, or your health breaking down.

But if we are fortunate enough to find a way to integrate our work into our home, then we don't have to think about balance between work and family so much as how we can weave the two together.

When I was young, my father ran a small bedspread manufacturing business with eight to ten employees. The business was his life. He worked all day and talked about it every night at dinner. We kids worked for him on weekends. As I look back, now I realize that the happiest moments of my father's life were during the short period of time that he had all three of his sons working with him in his business.

I think the loneliest businesspeople I see today are those whose children have no idea what they do. If you are able to teach your children what it is you do, what it is that they are economically dependent upon, and even better, if they can actually see you doing it and even participate in some meaningful way, then this destructive and alienating rift between work and home starts to dissolve.

There is actually something ironic about this. The U.S. started out as an agrarian nation of entrepreneurs where *everyone* was a small businessperson. The rise of the giant corporation, which my generation took for granted as the "normal" employment path, is really a historical anomaly. And it's rapidly slipping into the history books as we return to our entrepreneurial roots.

Chapter 10

Why Direct Selling

Of all the entrepreneurial opportunities available today, one of the most important is direct selling, also called "network marketing." The direct selling industry takes advantage of virtually every one of the trends we've just looked at, and is perfectly positioned to create many of these Next Millionaires.

> *The direct selling industry is perfectly positioned to create many of these Next Millionaires.*

Direct selling is actually the oldest form of selling. For most of human history, direct sellers were peddlers; as the primary distributors of tools and technology-based goods, they handled both the intellectual and physical aspects of distributing their wares. This began to shift with the development of third-party shipping and postal systems, which allowed direct sellers to concentrate more on intellectual distribution and simply take orders. In the nineteenth century, many direct sellers put down roots and became the general store and department store merchants of yesterday.

The whirlwind of technological advance over the last few decades has dramatically shifted the significance of this age-old direct selling function in the new economy. Here are a few statistics that will give you a sense of what the direct selling industry looks like today.

- Direct selling is a rapidly growing industry, with U.S. sales more than doubling in the last decade. U.S. sales in 2004 were more than $30 billion. Worldwide sales are nearly $100 billion.

- There are currently more than 15 million people involved in direct selling in the U.S., and nearly 50 million worldwide.

- Three quarters of the U.S. population (75 percent) have purchased goods or services through direct sales—more than the total number of those who have purchased through TV and Internet shopping combined.

- Nearly half the U.S. population (45 percent) say they want to buy from direct sellers.

- About 90 percent of all direct sellers operate their businesses part-time.

Data from the Direct Selling Association (www.dsa.org)

These figures, while exciting enough in their own right, reveal only the tip of the iceberg. For direct selling is yet one more example of a new and emerging industry, one that is perfectly positioned to take full advantage of all of the trends we've discussed up to this point. Today, the modern direct selling industry is poised to become the distribution method of choice for all new products and services.

> *The modern direct selling industry is poised to become the distribution method of choice for all new products and services.*

Direct Selling = Intellectual Distribution

In the '60s and early '70s, when the modern direct selling model was in its infancy, the business very much resembled having a store in your living room. No longer. From inexpensive long distance telephone and overnight carriers to video technology, home computers and now the Internet, the advance of technology in the past few decades has utterly transformed the business. And in the process, direct selling has become positioned perfectly to fill the technology gap.

Direct selling today is almost wholly *intellectual distribution*. When you as a direct seller discuss a product or service with a consumer, you typically don't actually hand over the product. You rely on UPS, FedEx or some other delivery service to ship the product to your customer. In the case of the many direct selling companies that sell services, such as legal protection, insurance, mortgages, investments and healthcare savings cards, the delivery is virtual. In fact, chances are good that the consumer will go online or call a 1-800 number and order the product or service direct from the company, which in turn credits the sale to you. You are completely out of the loop of physical delivery and serve a wholly educational function.

And there is no better vehicle anywhere for that kind of technology-gap-filling consumer education than direct selling.

I saw this first-hand in the early '90s, when I developed an educational software product line. Here was a product that could totally change a child's life—but telling people about it was far more expensive than producing it. We had a great new consumer product, but no way of telling the consumer it existed, and we were pretty much dead in the water—until we connected with a large network marketing company that took on the distribution of our product.

The companies that are prospering and will continue to prosper in direct selling are those that have adopted a model of having their independent distributors (also sometimes referred to as *representatives, associates* or *brokers*) focus almost entirely on intellectual distribution, teaching people about new products and services that will improve their lives. Those that really flourish will have some sort of unique or proprietary technology, product or service. And not just unique products or services, but efficacious ones—better than anything else out there.

Traditionally, where direct selling shines is in working with what are called "information-rich" products or services. This means products or services that people don't already know about, that are not widely known or understood, and that therefore need a significant amount of information to go with them. In practical terms, this often means products or services that are of especially high quality or high value: premium products or services.

The reason direct selling is especially well suited to premium products and services is they really need be sold by people who can explain them. Direct selling today is typically done person to person by someone who is also a user of the product or service. Unlike the car salesperson, electronics salesperson or clothing salesperson, the direct seller is an educated, enthusiastic, experienced user of the product or service you're asking about.

Direct selling is the perfect intellectual distribution business for today's economy. A home-based business doesn't require a storefront, warehouses, employees or massive back-office support operations. It only requires one person—*you*—willing to handle the educational component of the distribution process.

> *Direct selling is the perfect intellectual distribution business for today's economy.*

Direct Selling Is an "Active" Medium

I am often asked, "Since all these new products and services can be explained through the Internet now, won't online information replace all the people who were making their living explaining premium products?" In fact, during the waning years of the last century, there were some direct sellers who worried about just this problem.

They needn't have worried. As powerful as the Internet is, it hasn't replaced the one-to-one, personal function of the modern direct seller any more than did the television infomercials of the '80s and '90s, and it never will. The reason for this is one of the great limits of the technology. What's lacking with the Internet is the same thing that's lacking with television: it's a passive medium.

> *As powerful as the Internet is, it hasn't replaced the one-to-one, personal function of the modern direct seller, and it never will.*

Conventional advertising media are not effective at delivering what they call "intellectually challenging" information—which is a euphemism for "new ideas." This is because most of our information media today are forms of passive media. Television is a very passive medium for learning, so we can't really use it to teach new ideas. It's the same with newspapers. And to a great extent, the same is true of the Internet.

Think about how you watch television: you're sitting back, you're relaxed, on your couch; the last thing you want is to be challenged with new information. In fact, when you *do* see something that challenges you, something that disagrees with what you already know or think is true, what do you do? You change the channel. This is true of most of our media. Anytime you encounter something that challenges your view of the world, you change the station, turn to another page, or click the "BACK" button on your Internet browser.

When you go onto amazon.com, you may not know exactly what book you want, but you know you are looking for a book on a particular topic, or a particular type of book. You only go to learn about a product on the Internet when you want to learn about it—that is, you already know that something like it exists.

The reason direct selling works so uniquely well is that a one-to-one personal conversation is virtually the only way we actively learn—the only way we actually take in and start to consider brand new information about a completely new way of doing something.

And that is exactly what most of the new and emerging industries we're talking about need to do.

> *The reason direct selling works so uniquely well is that a one-to-one personal conversation is virtually the only way we actively learn.*

To put it another way: a person-to-person conversation is the most effective way, the most efficient way, and often the *only* way, to help bridge another person's technology gap. And because of this, the more technology grows, the more opportunity there will be for direct sellers, whom you might more accurately call *premium salespeople.*

The person who can teach or share with me a new way of doing something that's important to me is one of the most valuable people in my life. The investment advisor who shows me tools to help me maximize my wealth; the wellness advisor who introduces me to a product that will stop the ache in my knees; the financial services advisor who shows me a type of insurance that would fit my needs; these are people whose services I value.

I do business with people whose services might cost a bit more than what I might find on the Internet, but because they're always teaching me something or adding some value, they're more than worth it. The more new products come along, the more I need these people to advise me and educate me.

The Internet will soon take over the information function of teaching people things they already know they want to learn, and it will do that better, faster and in far more detail than ever before possible. But the really vital sales function of teaching people about things they *don't yet know* they want to learn—because they don't yet know they're available—will always be an educational model that will function best person-to-person.

It boils down to this: direct selling is the single most effective medium we have today, in the United States and around the world, for helping people close their technology gap. And since you know the sixth law of economic alchemy, you know what that means: it represents enormous economic potential.

> *Direct selling is the single most effective medium we have today, in the United States and around the world, for helping people close their technology gap.*

The Value of Residual Income

For most people, the only way you're every going to accumulate a significant amount of wealth is through passive income, which is another term for residual income. Residual income is income that continues to flow after the work that created it has been completed—income that is, in other words, *residue* remaining from the original effort.

> *For most people, the only way you're ever going to accumulate a significant amount of wealth is through passive income.*

The way you achieve a residual income flow is to create some sort of property, whether real or intellectual, that continues to yield cash flow to you year after year, long after the initial work is completed.

In real estate, you work hard to put together a good deal; once you have it completed and the property is in the condition you want, you get the income flow from it month after month. This was the original meaning of "royalties," because only the royalty (i.e., kings and queens) were in a position to own large amounts of land and derive residuals from the people dwelling on it.

In 1989, after I had been successful at real estate, I decided it was time to explore the world of intellectual property. I created my own publishing company and started to develop and acquire intellectual properties for publication on what would come to be called the Internet. Now, with a number of strong-selling books in print in 24 different languages, every time I go to the mailbox there's a check in there—what we now call "royalties."

This is a critical distinction, because it makes the difference between economic freedom and servitude. If your income consists exclusively of *compensation* income, then even if you work at a very high rate, such as a highly qualified lawyer, surgeon or corporate consultant, you are still tied to your work hours. Every day, you have to start over from scratch and earn all over again. If you stop working, you stop earning.

However, a residual income stream can continue, month after month, and conceivably for a lifetime. It is a classic example of economic alchemy at work: like the American farmers learning how to increase the productivity of their land, you are greatly increasing the economic productivity of the hours you spend so that they generate yield after yield for years to come.

This is one of the features I like best about direct selling. Not everyone is going to procure a significant piece of income-generating real estate, and not everyone is going to write a bestselling book. But direct selling provides an opportunity—open to absolutely anyone at all, regardless of background, specialized skills or accrued capital worth—to create a significant residual income.

> *Direct selling provides an opportunity—open to absolutely anyone at all, regardless of background, specialized skills or accrued capital worth—to create a significant residual income.*

In direct selling, the "property" that you develop is the network of direct sellers whose sales volume generates a commission to you, the creator of the network.

Direct Selling: A Personal Economic Alchemy Machine

One of the extraordinary things about direct selling is that because of its inherent structure, it is designed to work in your life as a force of economic alchemy itself. Let's look at what I mean by this:

You'll recall that in applying the formula for economic alchemy to your own life, your wealth is determined by your personal resources (P) and your personal technology (T). Direct selling is perfectly engineered to leverage and multiply both.

In this equation, your personal resources (P) are your individual relationships with people and the number of available work hours in your day. The structure of direct selling itself—that is, the way the organizations are constructed and the hierarchical, multi-tiered way you are compensated for others' efforts as well as your own—is itself an advanced technology that leverages your resources.

With a direct selling business, your own P is further maximized by recruiting and training others, who each start their own businesses and consume your company's products or services, generating additional business volume, a small percentage of which pays up to you. They also in turn recruit and train others, who do the same.

Thus, the *relationships you develop* and the *hours you work* are both powerfully leveraged by the multiplier effect of the direct selling technology itself.

This is ingenious—but that's not the most powerful aspect of this business.

One of the most valuable aspects of direct selling is that it is inherently designed to maximize your capacity to create wealth by *strongly developing your personal technology.*

Your personal technology (T) equals the skills you bring to your home-based business. This is where the direct selling industry sets itself apart from most other business opportunities. If you get involved in direct selling today, you are going to be exposed to trainings, materials, education, tools for developing belief systems and management systems (e.g., this book you are reading) that you're not likely to find anywhere else. They certainly don't teach these skills in high school or college.

> *If you get involved in direct selling today, you are going to be exposed to trainings, materials, education, tools for developing belief systems and management systems that you're not likely to find anywhere else.*

The skills you are likely to learn in direct selling may include computer and Internet proficiency, public speaking ability, leadership development, product knowledge, selling techniques, instructional ability, one-on-one communication techniques, and so forth. And this skill base is going to help you in everything else you do, whether it is a regular job or another form of entrepreneurial enterprise.

Direct selling companies are designed to handle for you the physical distribution of the products and services you sell—manufacturing, inventory, order processing, accounting, shipping, etc.—so that your primary business focus is on finding, recruiting and educating more customers. Moreover, since a direct selling company's success is directly dependent on your success, they also have a vested interest in helping you improve your technology.

This is a critical element in the technology of direct selling itself, and it represents a significant leap in development from most other forms of business.

For example, if someone were to sell you a franchise kit for a huge fee—and franchises can cost hundreds of thousands of dollars—they would have made their money and you would now have the risk. If you then failed, who would have lost? You.

But in direct selling, if I recruit you and then you fail, I am the one who loses. I lose all the time I spent recruiting you and training you. And all you've lost is the nominal cost to purchase your starter kit. Most direct selling companies subscribe to a code of ethics that says, "We will not pay you money or give you points for recruiting people; we only pay our people when the people in their organizations actually move product and sell something." Because of this, it is *structurally in the best interests of the people recruiting you* that you become as effective and as well trained as possible.

This is the opposite of the classic "dog eat dog," intensely competitive context of the traditional corporate work place. There is a saying people have in direct selling, that "you only win when you help others win." Because of the way the business is structured, it's more than a slogan or a statement of noble intent: it's a pragmatic strategy for success.

> *You only win when you help others win.*

And look what happens as you apply your ever-growing skills (T) to the new business relationships you are developing (P)—you're constantly dealing with new people and a greater diversity of people.

Helping other people make smart economic choices, create a business that they can operate from home, spend more time with their families and build a stream of residual income at the same time—and helping *so many different people* do this—offers its own rewards, far above and beyond the monetary rewards. And because of the huge spectrum of diversity one tends to see in direct selling, you are constantly improving the skills involved in working with different kinds of people. The nature of the business automatically compels you to develop your skills—and it develops the single most important skill you have: the ability to constantly learn and embrace new skills and new information.

Direct selling not only lets you build a better business: it also makes you a better entrepreneur.

Chapter 11

The Spiritual Nature of Business

In just the past few years, there has been a significant shift toward more intro-spection and examination of personal values, of what's truly important to us as human beings. People often attribute this to the tragedies of 9/11, the idea being that this renewed focus on the inward and the spiritual is a natural response to the ugliness and pain of the world outside.

In reality, I think it is just the opposite.

This accelerated emphasis on what's really important, on our spiritual values, didn't start in September of 2001. Our society was already moving in this direc-tion. And it is not a response to negativity; it is the natural response to success. The more we have achieved material aims, the better our lifestyles, the more we have secured our physical necessities and personal well-being, the more freedom we have felt to have the luxury of turning to the more important issues.

Economics is about the human quest for money. But in reality, it's not money we are after. It's really a quest for happiness, a quest for recognition, for all those things that we really want, which money is a vehicle to acquire, achieve or attain.

> *Economics is really a quest for happiness, a quest for recognition, for all those things that we really want, which money is a vehicle to acquire, achieve or attain.*

Money and the Meaning of Life

Spirituality has been the foundation of all of my work. To me, theology, spiritu-ality and economics are all the same thing. "Economics" is knowledge that will help you improve your life. If you were a farmer, back in the days when most of our great religions were founded, you wanted information that would give you more food, safe shelter and more free time to raise your children.

Our entrepreneurial side is not disconnected from our spiritual side. The act of being an entrepreneur is a theological act: it is a belief that God has given you the tools to go out, make money and take care of your family. That belief embraces the understanding that the better you do your job, the better off the world will be.

> *The act of being an entrepreneur is a theological act: it is a belief that God has given you the tools to go out, make money and take care of your family.*

We live in a world where we use our minds and our belief in our abilities to create wealth for everyone. This means that each person, if he understands these laws—which I consider to be the theological underpinnings of our economy—is able to go out and create unlimited wealth for himself. Furthermore, we live in a world where the more you succeed, not only do you grow wealthier, but everyone else in the world also grows wealthier, because in today's world, we succeed by serving.

If you ask most entrepreneurs why they do what they do, chances are good they'll say, "Oh, I love making money! I love *having* money! I love being financially independent and being able to take care of my family."

And all those things are undoubtedly true. But if you actually spend a day in their office and watch them at work, you'll see something else going on. You'll see them working away, building their businesses and creating wealth…and you'll see the joy they get from serving others. You'll see that what drives all that creativity and industry is the fact that they love people.

People who make money and create wealth by owning and building their own businesses love other people. They love taking their wisdom and experience and sharing it with people right out of school, sharing it with colleagues and customers. They love having people around them with whom they can share the benefits of their experience.

They'll tell you that it's all about making money. But it's really about touching the lives of other human beings in a positive way. It's about making the world a better place.

> *People who make money and create wealth by owning and building their own businesses love other people.*

The Value of Having a Job You Love

This may come as a surprise, but one of the keys to success in today's fast-changing economy is having a job that you love. Why? Because that's the only sure way to create satisfied, happy customers—and in the new economy, the customer truly is king and queen.

Keeping your focus on your customer has always been a key component in creating a business that excels. In the twenty-first century, it's not just a good idea, it's critical. Consumers today are not only far more educated about the choices available to them in a particular product or service, they also have far higher standards for the transaction itself. Customer service expectations are higher than ever.

When I am building a new business, here's how I start my typical day: the first thing I do in the morning is dial my company's 1-800 number and pretend I'm a customer! (I use all sorts of other names, so they don't know it's me.) If the number isn't answered till the fourth ring, or I don't like the answer I get to my question, then I know exactly where we need to improve, and I sit down and write my memos for the day.

Why do I do this? Because it's so easy for all of us to be caught up with our suppliers and all the people we work with. It's easy to lose track of the reality of our business if we don't spend time with the customer. Keeping the customer in mind is one of the most important factors in the success of your business—of *any* business. When you do, everything else will tend to fall into place. If I didn't start every day as a customer of my own business, I know I wouldn't stand a chance of being competitive.

What makes any business more successful than any other? It produces more happiness and more satisfaction for its customers than its competitors do. In this evermore competitive world, your customers *need you to enjoy* bringing them those products and services—or they'll go elsewhere.

For you to enjoy that, you have to care about them. For you to care about them, you have to love what you do. In virtually every field, you have to love what you do in order to achieve great success in it. Your customers are not going to want to buy something from someone who doesn't really want to provide it for reasons other than money.

The Spiritual Value of Direct Selling

In the last chapter, we looked at many of the practical and economic advantages of having your own home-based, direct selling business. As you've no doubt already surmised, these strengths also translate into tremendous personal and lifestyle advantages.

For example, we looked at the difficulties and challenges of balancing work and family, and how much more rewarding and practical it is to find a way to *integrate* work and family. In direct selling, I see a more substantial progression towards a seamless weaving together of work and family than in perhaps any other sector of the economy.

One thing I like so much about direct selling is that its practitioners are really teaching spiritual values (even if they don't call it that), as much as they are teaching about pure business. In the act of sitting down with someone, one-on-one, the direct seller has an unusual opportunity to teach others about unlimited wealth: that we are not running out of resources—that when they succeed, they are creating more wealth for everyone.

Sadly, this is not a prevalent view in our social environment, especially in the last few years as we've entered a time of more turmoil. In too many sectors of society, there is a prevalent undercurrent of pessimism, cynicism and fear about the state of the world. As I said in the introduction to this book, we have seen overwhelming evidence in the past decade of the economy of growing abundance and incredible opportunity in which we live.

But people have forgotten this evidence and lost touch with this preponderance of good news. It's our job to bring this back—and that is something that direct sellers do almost without thinking. It's that inherent in the design, the technology, of direct selling itself.

Another reason direct selling is such a positive social and spiritual force in our culture right now is its emphasis on inclusivity.

The prosperity I'm predicting for the years ahead is going to be even more selective than it's been the last 15 years. In other words, those people who are on the right part of the technology curve—those people making DVDs instead of VHS tapes, so to speak, people distributing wellness and prevention versus symptomatic illness care; people learning how to use the Internet and new technology versus older technologies—these are the people whose prosperity is going to increase.

Even though, in the macroeconomic picture, we are creating more and more economic opportunity for all, these rapid changes are going to create more temporary displacement than ever, which means that the disparity in society between the haves and the have-nots will become more aggravated, not less.

Direct selling offers a very real solution to millions who stand to suffer from being on the wrong end of each technological shift. As a direct seller, you can offer the same opportunity you are taking advantage of to anyone; they need no college degree, no specialized training, no professional credential nor specific résumé. They need only be willing to learn—and with that, people from across the widest imaginable spectrum can become self-employed entrepreneurs, fulfill a service of intellectual distribution for others, and begin to realize their economic potential—and even create the basis for a residual income in the process!

> *Direct selling offers a very real solution to millions who stand to suffer from being on the wrong end of each technological shift.*

More than any other business, direct selling starts with the core: not with the product or the service, but with the process of helping other people, by teaching other people how to succeed, regardless of their education or what business or field they've been in. This is why I say that at its heart, building a direct selling business is a theological act every bit as much as it is an economic act.

We live during the first time in history when people have made a deliberate disconnect between economics and theology: "I do this for business and I do that for church." In so doing, people completely miss the point that what will make them successful in business are precisely those values they learned in their church, synagogue or mosque.

More importantly, people miss the economic concept that in this world of unlimited resources, one person's gain is a gain for all people in all of society. It is a great motivating force to help you understand your faith better. We live in a time where people think we should separate them; I believe that we should combine them.

Business is about serving other people. The better you are at giving people something that improves their lives, the more successful you are, and the more money you make. That, to me, is serving God: doing the best job you can at serving other people. I know of no business that exemplifies this principle as well as direct selling.

> *Business is about serving other people. The better you are at giving people something that improves their lives, the more successful you are, and the more money you make.*

Chapter 12

Your Economic Wellness

At various points throughout this book, I have mentioned direct selling as an especially vital and valuable way to capitalize on the many trends we've looked at. Now, before we wrap all this together and look at your own personal "economic wellness," I'd like to tell you a little bit about how I came to be connected to this fascinating industry.

As I wrote in the very beginning of this book, most of the financial and business community greeted my 1990 book *Unlimited Wealth,* in whose pages I first put forth my theory of economic alchemy, with reactions ranging from polite indifference to outright ridicule. As the decade unrolled and my predictions began proving accurate, that obviously changed—but there were those who got the message loud and clear and responded to it immediately. Those in the direct selling community were among that perceptive vanguard.

Direct sellers were quick to grasp the significance of what I'd written, and I began to become acquainted with many of them and how they operated their business. But it didn't stop there.

At the time, I was not aware of the direct selling business, and certainly had no opinion of them. I did not seek them out—but they sought me out, because they saw that what I was saying completely bore out their own experience. Economic alchemy and *Unlimited Wealth* explained, demystified, illuminated and validated the direct selling model.

As I continued to meet and interact with more members of the direct selling community, they got to know my work—and I got to know theirs. In the process, I also got to know *them.*

Over the past 15 years, I have spoken before hundreds of thousands of direct sellers. I've spoken before their assemblies and conferences, stood for hours in book-signing lines and had personal conversations with them, listening to them tell me about their experiences. I've gathered a broad and rich sense of who they are and what they do.

I have also had the opportunity to get to know several hundred of the top achievers in the profession, both field and corporate, on a personal level. I have become close friends with quite a few, vacationed with them, gone snowboarding with them, had them stay at my home.

I've also counseled CEOs, coached distributors, and worked with many of these companies on a professional level, as well as speaking before the Direct Selling Association (DSA).

When you read my various recommendations, suggestions and comments (for example, in the section below on "What Should I Look For in a Direct Selling Company?"), know that I am grateful for the experience and wisdom of many of the masters in this field, and that it is their insights that inform these passages.

What these experiences have shown me is that direct selling provides an unparalleled opportunity for millions of people to take responsibility for their own economic wellness, create long-term financial stability and even realize significant wealth, even while enriching the lives of untold numbers of others.

It is a vehicle through which many of you reading these words will make the world a better place, even as you become one of the Next Millionaires.

> *Direct selling provides an unparalleled opportunity for millions of people to take responsibility for their own economic wellness, create long-term financial stability and even realize significant wealth, even while enriching the lives of untold numbers of others.*

The Concept of Economic Wellness

The new and emerging wellness industry is built on a new paradigm, which says, "Rather than wait until we become sick tomorrow, why not take steps to increase our wellness today? And what's more, if we do that, maybe we'll also greatly increase the chances that we won't get sick in the first place."

It is a preventive model: proactive instead of reactive. And in these days of rapid change, it makes sense to adopt a similar strategy for your economic life.

Rather than wait until your job becomes obsolete and you become one of the displacement unemployment statistics, or until you find yourself in a business environment where you are being left behind, why not be proactive?

Why wait until there is a traffic accident that bars your way to where you want to go? Why not look for a better way *now,* while the roads are still clear?

You *can* be in control of your health. And you *can* be in control of your wealth. You can and must take charge of your *economic wellness.*

Where and How Should I Work?

In this chapter, we'll look at strategies for preserving and investing your wealth as you earn it. But these serve your wealth something like the way exercise programs serve your health: they build on it, but they are not at the core of it.

At the core of your health is *your diet:* what you eat every day.

And at the core of your wealth is *your work:* what you *do* every day.

In order to take control of your wealth and steer yourself into becoming one of the Next Millionaires, it's essential that you invest the work hours you have available every day as productively as possible.

Is your work in a new and emerging industry? Or does it in some way serve, interact with or derive benefit from a new and emerging industry? For example, if you are an accountant, should you consider focusing on clients within specific industries that are poised for massive growth?

How well are you managing your *technology gap?* Are you continuously seeking out new and better ways of doing things in your work? Are you continually seeking out new and better sources for the latest information about your industry, and keeping yourself as educated and well-informed as you can?

Are you fully taking advantage of the Internet as a way to build your business?

Are you fully taking advantage of the Internet as a way to reach, inform and educate potential customers?

Are you fully taking advantage of the Internet as a way to stay informed about the latest developments, both worldwide and locally, that may have an impact on your business?

Does your business allow you to fulfill the role of intellectual distribution—informing consumers about new and better products that can improve the quality of their lives, but which they don't know about yet?

What about your own personal economic alchemy?

Do you have a complete inventory of all the people you know, people whose trust you've earned, who would return a phone call? If not, this may be a good time to sit down and create such an inventory: this is your personal resource, the (P) in the economic alchemy equation, and is your equivalent of land, gold, steel and oil upon which the millionaires of the past built their fortunes.

Are there any areas in your *basic skills* (reading, writing, speaking, calculation and processing information) that you could afford to improve upon?

What about your *functional skills,* that is, whatever specialized skills you have picked up in your experiences to date? Make an inventory of these skills and consider each one in turn: is there some new and creative way you can apply any of these skills to multiply your wealth-building capacity?

Are you doing something you love? As long as you're taking inventory, this is a good time to sit down and list your passions, strengths and experiences. What kind of work gives you the most joy? What have you loved doing most in the past? How can you take what you love most and turn it into an entrepreneurial business?

In your work, are you maximizing your productivity by applying the best technology you can find to the resources in your business?

For example, if you are in the direct selling business, the equation of economic alchemy is crucial to your success. Many direct sellers miss this crucial fact and end up working very hard but not achieving all the success they could. Yet those who are extremely successful understand and apply this equation masterfully. How?

Here is an example:

It's not just how many distributors you recruit that determines your success, it's also the productivity of each distributor.

In other words, how well you are applying technology to make sure those distributors you do recruit are as well trained, as well informed and as well equipped as possible, matters far more than just the sheer numbers of people you bring into your organization. In the equation $W = P \times T$, the number of distributors you recruit is P—but how well you train and equip them is T.

Here is another example:

It's not just how many hours per week you put into your direct selling business that determines your income, but also how you use those hours.

You could devote 40 hours a week to recruiting and recruiting, and yet still build only a fraction of the wealth you could build if you were spending half that time but putting a good portion of it into the highest quality training and tool-building.

When Should I Quit My Job?

In today's and tomorrow's economy, one of the best things you can do to ensure that you are part of the powerful current of new wealth creation is to become an individual entrepreneur or independent contractor.

A number of years ago I wrote a book titled, *Should You Quit Before You're Fired?* The answer I give to that question is generally, "Yes!"

To be more specific, my advice is to *make sure you are always working in a business where you can use and leverage your skills for the highest return.*

How do you know when is the right time to quit your job, move into a new area or switch careers? There's no right formula for everyone, but I have a formula that I have always followed. If you look at my résumé, it's somewhat unusual in that I've embarked on a new career every three to five years. How did I know when it was time to move?

I call it my 51 Percent Rule.

I advise people to keep a log or record of the time they spend involved in their work. Whether you work at home or at an office or both, write down the hours you work, dividing them into two categories: hours you spend learning something new, and hours you spend doing something you already know how to do.

Your first day on new job, chances are good that 100 percent of your hours are spent learning. The next day, perhaps 95 percent of your time is learning, because you already know what to do in certain aspects of the job from what you learned yesterday.

Let's say that by the end of three months, 30 percent what you do is repetition of what you've already learned, and 70 percent is still learning. A week later, that 70 percent might go back up to 85 percent, because your boss comes in with a new computer system or program for you to learn, or perhaps he or she moves you to a new aspect of the job, so now your learning ratio goes back up.

At some point, whether it's after six months, or eight months, or a year or even more, you will reach the point where you are spending over half your time doing what you already know how to do.

That's when you quit.

In other words, I'm recommending that you should always be in a business where you are spending *at least 51 percent* of the hours you work learning new things and improving your skills. Why? Because you're investing in your personal technology. Remember W = P x T? By following the 51 Percent Rule, you are always increasing your T—which means you are always increasing your ability to create new wealth.

And the truth is, if you're involved in a job where an employee such as yourself is spending more than half your time doing the grunt work of repetition, the job you're working for is on its way out anyway. There is no longer time for businesses that don't grow and learn and adapt and change. Technology is growing too fast.

What Should I Look For in a Direct Selling Company?

Let's say you've decided to devote some part-time hours to starting and building a direct selling business. Among the hundreds of companies out there, how do you choose which one is right for you?

THE MOST IMPORTANT FACTOR

Fortunately, the single most important factor that determines how successful you will be in direct selling is a factor that is under your complete control: that factor is *you*.

> *The most important factor that determines how successful you will be in direct selling is you.*

One of the most intriguing and powerful features of the direct selling industry is that, perhaps more than in any other mode of business, your rewards are directly proportional to the quality of your own efforts.

This is a two-edged sword, of course. On the one hand, it means that there is no artificial, arbitrary or unfair limitation imposed, no "glass ceilings" or discriminatory criteria for success. It is a truly level playing field, open to all. On the other hand, this also means that you are a true entrepreneur: nothing will happen unless you make it happen!

How much you work, how hard you work, but especially how smart you work, is the number one determinant of the level of wealth you will create in this business.

Beyond yourself, the three most important factors in your direct selling success are: the nature of the product or service, the strength of the company and its financial opportunity; and the particular team you will be working with.

THE PRODUCT OR SERVICE

Here is the cardinal rule of direct selling: *You should absolutely use and believe in the products or services you sell.*

As we saw earlier, direct selling is especially well suited to "information-rich" products and services, in other words, products that have a story to tell. The most successful direct selling products are often those that would not do well sitting on a retail shelf at a Wal-Mart store, because they are products people don't already know about: there is a significant amount of information needed to create a market for them, and it's not the kind of information that moves best through a passive information source like television, magazine ads or even the Internet.

> *You should absolutely use and believe in the products or services you sell.*

This is the kind of paradigm-altering, life-improving information that is best communicated person to person—which is exactly why direct selling works so well.

Because the essence of direct selling is the person-to-person conversation, your own personal belief in the validity of value of the product is essential. Here is an excellent litmus test: Ask yourself, "Would I buy this product or service if I were not part of the sales organization?" If the answer is, "No," think twice about the opportunity.

While there are many direct selling companies who work in the area of wellness, this is by no means the only option. You'll recall I successfully marketed a line of educational software through a direct selling organization. There are direct selling companies that offer every imaginable sort of product and service, from wellness to educational products to home products to financial and legal services to insurance to cosmetics to apparel and everything in between. The great entrepreneur W. Clement Stone once famously stated, "What the mind of man can conceive and believe, he can achieve." Today, if your mind can conceive it, there is probably a direct selling company somewhere selling it!

At the same time, you have the luxury of choice. As you look for the product or service that fits best with your ambitions, examine every product you explore against the yardstick of economic alchemy and today's environment of rapid change and exploding technological development.

Are they me-too products with a "business as usual" message, or is this a product or service that lives on the cutting edge? Is there something distinctly new and unique about it? Is it a new and better way of doing something? Does it improve people's lives?

THE COMPANY AND OPPORTUNITY

As a direct seller, you enjoy an unusual relationship with the corporation, one that offers all the benefits of being a self-employed entrepreneur, together with many of the benefits of being allied with an established company.

As a direct seller, you are not an employee of the company, but an independent contractor. Your income, for example, is reported on a 1099 (miscellaneous income), not on a W-2 (wage income), and no income tax or FICA deductions are taken; it is paid as pure commission income. This also means that yours is a completely voluntary position: you are literally your own boss, and this translates into many of the "freedom" benefits that direct sellers are so fond of touting (and rightly so): freedom to set your own hours, to work how you want, when you want, with whom you want, etc.

Direct sellers are also fond of saying that you are in business "for yourself, but not by yourself," and this is equally true. While you are not an employee, your business relies strongly on your partnership with the corporation. They not only produce the product or supply the service, take and fulfill orders through their web site or 1-800 phone lines, keep track of all orders and payments and pay out all commissions and bonuses. They also provide an extraordinary amount of support, in the form of research and new product development, preparation and distribution of promotional materials, field training, logistical support, and a great deal more.

> *When you choose a company, you are choosing a business partner.*

In short, when you choose a company, you are choosing a business partner. How do you evaluate your prospective partner?

There are basic features to look for that will help determine a legitimate, reasonably solid opportunity from an obviously substandard company. For example, with any legitimate company these days, your start-up costs will be nominal, with all other purchases for inventory or materials being optional. All income is earned based on the actual sale of products and services to the end user; in other words, there are no monies paid for the sheer act of recruiting ("head-hunting" fees). And there will be a product buy-back policy, so that the company will allow you to return unsold inventory in saleable condition, purchased within, say, the past six to twelve months, usually for 90 percent of the price you paid.

For more information on such basic criteria, refer to the web site of the Direct Selling Association (www.dsa.org). The DSA, which is the trade organization that represents direct selling corporations, also publishes a list of member companies; all DSA member companies pledge to uphold and abide by the DSA Code of Ethics.

Beyond these basic criteria, you'll want to assess the background, experience and strength of the corporate principals. What is their track record? How long has this company been in business, and what businesses have they run prior to this one?

Direct selling is a business vehicle especially well suited for global expansion. What is the company's present international exposure, and what are their plans for further international expansion?

How committed are they to providing the best in information, training and education? One the greatest strengths of direct selling lies in the extent to which it develops you personally and both broadens and deepens your skills.

What is their technology gap like? Is it using the latest, best technology? What does its Internet presence tell you?

You will probably find reams of information about the company on their web site, as well as in their printed and audio-video literature. In addition to company-generated material, before you decide upon a company to affiliate with, it is wise to talk with others who've had direct experience with this company to verify the information and get as much perspective as you can.

Remember, you're not simply affiliating with a supplier—you're selecting a partner.

THE TEAM

In practice, a direct selling organization usually grows through a model very similar to the mentor/apprentice model that craftsmen, artists and entrepreneurs have used for centuries. The person or people who recruit you into a direct selling organization are there to serve the function of orientation, education, training and guidance. In other words, to show you the ropes.

While the people who directly recruit you derive economic benefit from your activity, that benefit doesn't stop there. The people who recruited *them* are also compensated from the sales in your growing organization, as are the people who recruited *them,* and so forth through a number of generations. Consequently, the team of independent distributors who stand to gain from your being as well trained as possible may include quite a handful of people. And these people, even more than the corporate staff, are your in-the-trenches team of partners.

As with the company itself, you'll want to evaluate this team's level of commitment to making sure you are thoroughly trained. What are their skills, track record, use of technology, etc.?

Have they been successful? It isn't necessary that the person who recruits you has already achieved the kind of wealth you are looking for. After all, he or she may have preceded you into this organization by a matter of only days, weeks or months. But it's helpful to know that *someone* in this organization has already been successful doing what you are about to do. Are there people already in the organization, people who have preceded you in building with this particular company, who have achieved the kinds of financial goals you have?

THE FINAL CRITERION

While it's important to do your best to make a wise selection of product or service, company and team, there's no need to shop forever for the "perfect opportunity." There are literally dozens and even hundreds of good companies to choose from, and you should with a reasonable amount of due diligence be able to find a situation that will suit you well.

Then it's time to get started and start learning and building. For how long? Therein lies the final criterion.

Because there are so many examples of "ordinary people" achieving extraordinary economic results in direct selling, newcomers to the business sometimes embark on their new career with the misguided idea that they should be able to achieve massive incomes in a very short time. This is not only an unlikely expectation, but also an unwise one.

One hallmark of a mature, high quality direct selling company is that the personnel, whether corporate or distributor field, will present the income opportunity as a serious commitment that will yield reasonable results when pursued with commitment for a reasonable length of time. It is not, in other words, a vehicle for "getting rich quick." However, it is most definitely a vehicle for getting rich.

So, how long does it take? It's of course impossible to say, but most responsible direct sellers will advise that you should expect to put in reasonable, consistent effort (usually part-time) for from one to several years, in that amount of time be able to create the basis for a significant stream of long-term residual income.

The specifics and particulars will vary from situation to situation and individual to individual. The principle, however, is a constant for everyone: the final criterion for a solid direct selling situation is your commitment to work at it, diligently and seriously, with the commitment of an entrepreneur. The rewards are well worth it.

Where Should I Invest?

No matter how savvy you are in building your own entrepreneurial business, whether it is in direct selling, marketing your own skills as a free-lance agent, or building another type of business, the adage "nothing is forever" is as true about earning an income as it ever was. Actually, it's more so.

In a world where the pace of technological change has accelerated to warp speeds and the markets shift and transform so swiftly we can barely follow them, it is impossible to select a form of gainful employment (even self-employment) and expect that income flow to continue throughout your life. The world simply changes too fast.

More than ever before, how you invest what you earn is a critical part of your economic wellness.

There are many ways to invest, each with their strengths and weaknesses, and it is not the purpose of this book to offer extensive insight or counsel on any one of them. What I do want to offer here is a set of guidelines for how to set your *investment priorities.*

There are three broad types of investing, and they are, in descending order of importance: investing in yourself; investing for safety; and investing for growth.

THE MOST IMPORTANT INVESTMENT

The most important investment is *investing in yourself.* Before you invest in anything else, exhaust the possibilities of investing in your own business first. Why? There are two reasons.

> *Before you invest in anything else, exhaust the possibilities of investing in your own business first.*

First, because when you invest in your own business, you really can't lose. Even when do you lose, you gain. Let me explain.

If you invest $5,000 in the stock market, and you lose the $5,000, it's simply gone, period. But if you put that same $5,000 into your business, what happens? Let's say you purchase a new machine; or you invest in a new software program, marketing materials such as books, CDs and DVDs, or advanced training for yourself, or both.

Two things may happen. One, the investment pays off. Your business' earning power increases, and you're more than $5,000 ahead—way more, if you factor in future years of growth at this new level or higher.

Or, it doesn't pay off. The machine doesn't work as advertised. You don't apply the training. Whatever the reason, you lose the money. But you learn.

When we lose money on something, we stop, think and analyze. We're on guard the next time we're confronted with that same situation or thinking of making a similar investment. When you lose money in your business, you earn more in terms of your experience that will in turn make you more next year, the following year and the rest of your life. In fact, when you invest in your own business, the more you lose, the more you learn.

Our learning experiences come primarily from our mistakes, not our good choices. Our good choices are good too, of course, and we move forward with them—but we don't learn anywhere near as much as when we make mistakes. And the experience gained is nearly always worth more, in real long-term dollar terms, than the money lost.

The second reason your own business is the most important investment is that, if you are following the advice in this book, you have created a business that will continue to provide income for you into the future on a residual basis.

Whether it's a direct selling business, a portfolio of real estate holdings, some sort of intellectual property (such as writing a book), when you create a business asset that continues to produce income for you after you've completed the initial work to build it, you are earning a residual income, potentially for the rest of your life.

And any money you invest into building a residual is the wisest investment of all.

INVESTING FOR SAFETY

After investing in yourself and your own business, if you then want to invest some of your earnings in a way that preserves them for the future—in other words, a way that keeps those earnings safe—then you invest in tax-deferred vehicles.

This is exactly what most people miss when they go to invest. They think, "I'll go invest where it makes the highest return"—but what you want is the highest return *after taxes*.

For this, I recommend you set up and completely maximize your 401(k), your IRA, HSA and any other tax-deferred vehicles available to you.

All these vehicles have the same thing in common: the money you invest is deducted from your gross income for that year, so you pay no income taxes on that portion of your earnings. That means that you're investing up to twice the money that you would have to invest anywhere else, if you were investing in after-tax dollars.

Compile a list of every tax-deferred vehicle you have available to your situation, and stockpile away every dollar you can into these accounts. Twenty or thirty thousands dollars put away into a series of these accounts will quickly accumulate to millions of dollars over a working lifetime.

People often ask me, "What traits will make me wealthy? What's most important to teach my children, if I want them to become successful and wealthy?"

I often reply that the single most important trait or quality for financial success is not a business trait, but a spiritual one: the capacity to *willingly delay gratification*.

> *The single most important trait for financial success is the capacity to willingly delay gratification.*

This is the essence of saving. Saving is what distinguishes us from animals. Like all animals, we have desires for immediate gratification; we want food, happiness, sex, joy. The essence of civilization, of becoming a more spiritual being, is being able to say, "My desire for future greater gain is stronger than my immediate need for gratification. I have money, but I'm not going to drink it, spend it or run off on a vacation: I'm going to save it to make my family's life better in the future."

When I look at successful people, the thing I always see they have in common is this ability to exercise the discipline it takes not to spend or consume everything they earn right away, but consciously to build for the future. It is a kind of faith: faith that by taking certain acts of self-denial today, I'll be creating a better future. In fact, this is the only universal trait I've found shared by all successful people I've ever met.

Whether you are an employee of a corporation and planning to create a second, entrepreneurial income stream, or are already a full-time entrepreneur yourself, you need a back-up plan so you will be able to support yourself and your family for one, two or three years in the event of a sudden unforeseen shift in your income.

Part of the reason I had such a successful career over the five years I worked for Citibank was that I saved so much of my salary in the first six months that I knew I could be fired and have enough to live for six months while I looked for another job. This gave me enough confidence so that I could begin to take risks that I wouldn't have taken otherwise—risks that could have blown up my face, but which ultimately led to promotions and greater opportunities.

In the past, we would think of a salary from a job as a sort of annuity: it would keep coming in year after year. That is now an antiquated viewpoint we can no longer afford to have.

The way to do this is to stockpile funds in tax-deferred vehicles, so that you are not taxed on the income.

THE SMARTEST STOCK INVESTMENT

So, what if you're already investing solidly in your own business, you have your tax-deferred vehicles in place, and now you want to invest some of your remaining income into the stock market or in third-party companies?

Here is my advice: it only makes sense to do so if you're going to make significant money. And the only real way to make money in the stock market is to have an *edge* over other people; in other words, you have to have knowledge others don't have.

There is only one legal and ethical way to do that: invest only in companies that are in businesses *that you know about* from your personal experience.

> *Invest only in companies that are in businesses that you know about from your personal experience.*

This is not knowledge that you read about on Yahoo or follow in *The Wall Street Journal* or *The New York Times;* everybody else has that information, too. This is knowledge that you have gained by working in a particular field and knowing the products and services in that specialized field like the back of your hand.

You know more about these businesses, from your view on Main Street, than the professional analysts know from their view on Wall Street. And ultimately, a company's value on Wall Street *depends* on its value on Main Street.

Let's say you're an optometrist and want to invest. Make a list of all the machines you use in your work. Follow those stocks. You'll know whether those machines are good or bad or if they're going to continue selling *before* the people on Wall Street do after the end of the year from combing the annual reports.

Compile a list of the companies in your industry that make the products that you use. How well are they doing? Who is doing it better? This is where you have your natural edge and you should take advantage of it. There is no reason to give your money blindly to someone who says, "I can invest and make you more money." You should be doing it yourself.

Why Do I Work?

Throughout this book, we've touched on a whole range of reasons that we work, benefits that we derive from our work, that go beyond making money and creating wealth.

We know, for example, that in the course of engaging in the problem-solving, entrepreneurial process itself, we learn. We learn new skills, and in so doing, we hone our very ability to learn. We've even made for ourselves a rule: the moment we find ourselves spending less than half our work time learning something new, it's time to move on to more uncharted territory!

We know that we can create not only a good flow of income today, but also a basis for residual or "passive" income, which is itself a source of continuing wealth that in time can free us from the necessity of trading hours for dollars.

We know that with wise savings and investment, taking advantage of the new and better regulatory environment for entrepreneurs, we can build long-term financial security for our families and ourselves.

And we've seen how we can use the context of a home-based business to shift the relationship of home and family, so that instead of having it be a constant battle, trade-off or compromise, we can integrate both aspects of our lives, creating a richer experience of both family and business.

We know that one of the best business strategies is to make sure we're doing something we love, and that our businesses are expressions of our passions and highest values.

There is yet another reason, beyond all of these personal reasons, that we work, and personally, I believe it is our highest and strongest reason.

We work to build a better world.

> ### *We work to build a better world.*

I hear much talk these days about the decline of community—but like the economic pessimism we touched on at the very beginning of this book, I believe this viewpoint is myopic and inaccurate. In fact, I see just the opposite happening. I see a tremendous leap forward in the development and enrichment of the entire idea of community.

In the past, your "community" meant your physical community—the city or town where you were born and the block, street or neighborhood where you grew up. You were locked into that city or town with that same socio-demographic group. If you were poor, everyone was poor. If you were middle class, everyone was middle class. We defined community by where you were from. That's what community *was*.

Today that's all changed.

Today community means the *way you think*. Just as your job is no longer determined by your last name or place of origin, you yourself are no longer defined by your name or where you're from. Today you are defined by what you do and the choices you've made, not the circumstances in which you were born. You find your community among other professionals and entrepreneurs who do the same thing you do, who share the same values and dedication. You choose your community—in fact, just as you create your wealth, you *create* your community, by virtue of your values and common interests. I believe we are far better off than being locked into the neighborhoods to which we were born.

Years ago, I wrote a book titled *The Theology of Economics: God Wants You To Be Rich*. The premise of the book was that when you go out into the world and successfully earn money, you are helping other people, adding value to society, and contributing to the betterment of the world.

Abraham discovered that in laying claim to a piece of property, putting down roots and developing it, he could make far better use of his God-given gifts and help raise the quality of life and living for all around him. Today, the piece of property we stake out, the "place" where we put down our entrepreneurial roots, roll up our sleeves and begin to ply our ingenuity, is more likely to be a business located somewhere in cyberspace than a plot of physical ground. The resources we start with are not gold, grain, herds and acres, but relationships, experiences, information and our precious waking hours. Nonetheless, we are again becoming a nation of farmers, independent and pioneering entrepreneurs who till the soil of our imaginations and work together to produce ever greater yields of new crops, the variety and nature of which our ancestors would scarcely have had the vocabulary to dream.

We live in a time of discovery, where we are finding the human mind has far more capacity and ability than we ever imagined. The accelerating path of technology and ingenuity has finally revealed the process of economic alchemy in plain evidence before us, and shown us the truth that there is no limit to our resources, our technology, or our wealth, because these are all created in the God-given mind—and that mind, like its source, is without limits.

Afterword

One rainy day, a religious man sat in his study reading when his neighbor came by with a truck.

"A terrible flood is coming!" his neighbor exclaimed. "We're all evacuating. We've just got room for you on our truck!"

"Don't worry about me," the man replied. "I'll be all right: God will provide."

The flood waters began to rise; the man's house began to flood, and before long, he was forced up to the second floor, where he saw some other neighbors furiously rowing by in a boat just outside his bedroom window.

"Get in our boat!" they called to him, "The floodwaters are still rising! You'll be drowned!"

But the man remained calm. "Don't worry about me, I'll be all right," he told them. "God will provide."

After another hour, the floodwaters had completely covered the pious man's house, driving him up to the rooftop, where he clung to the chimney. He noticed an approaching helicopter: a rescue team had spotted him and now hovered over his disappearing house, unrolling a rope ladder.

"CLIMB UP!" shouted the rescue team leader.

But the man shook his head and waved them on. "IT'S ALL RIGHT!" he shouted back, "GO ON WITHOUT ME! GOD WILL PROVIDE!"

The helicopter left without him.

The water continued to rise and the man drowned.

Later, as he made his way through the Pearly Gates and into Heaven, he met God. The man shook his hands in despair and cried out, "Hey, what happened out there? You really let me down! I had faith that you would save me! Where were you?"

"Where was I?" replied God. "I sent you a truck. I sent you a boat. I sent you a helicopter. Tell me—what were you waiting for?!"

Don't wait for the water to cover your home; don't procrastinate until you find yourself hugging the chimney. There are amazing vehicles waiting for you, to transport you out of the flood and lead you to economic safety—to help you become one of *The Next Millionaires.*

The next step is up to you.

Selected Quotes

"Today there are at least ten million more people who will shrug off the pessimism and malaise of the times, who will grasp and ride the surging currents of new wealth creation over the next ten years to become the Next Millionaires."

"Our economy is in the middle of its greatest growth spurt in history."

"The Internet represents one of the greatest economic revolutions in history—and it's just getting started."

"In today's world, working for yourself is actually the safer route, and working for a corporation has become the riskier proposition."

"The individual entrepreneur today is often far more competitive than the big corporation."

"Home-based businesses are one of the fastest-growing segments in our economy, and that trend will only continue, as the age of the corporation, which began barely a century ago, now gives way to the age of the entrepreneur."

"Greater and greater diversity of skills, greater and greater specialization, leads to more and more trade. Increased trade leads to a further increase in wealth for all involved."

"Our wealth is rewarded directly in proportion to the number of people with whom we are willing to share."

"The kind of tunnel vision that said the planets revolve around the earth, that declared the earth was flat, that proclaimed Abraham nuts to try and 'own' and cultivate land—is alive and well and with us today, crippling the prevalent understanding of wealth and the economy."

"Economics today is where medicine was 200 years ago: it has its medicines and procedures, and they sometimes appear to work (although they sometimes kill the patient in the process), but there is no clear theory to explain why they work, or don't. We are without a working theory to explain what we see happening around us."

"All my work over the past three decades has revolved around the task of debunking the myth of scarcity".

"We have a proven antidote to war: free trade."

"Free trade is the engine that fuels the growth of wealth."

"The first law of economic alchemy says that there are no resources to run out of, because all resources are inventions of the human mind."

"The second law of economic alchemy says that the supply of any given resource, at any given moment, depends upon the technology with which you find it, extract it and use it."

"$W = P \times T$ Wealth (W) equals the physical resources available (P) multiplied by the technology available (T)."

"The third law of economic alchemy says that the advance of technology is determined by the speed with which you exchange information."

"The fourth economic law of alchemy says that technology doesn't merely help fill a need—technology actually determines what constitutes a 'need.'"

"The fifth law of economic alchemy simply says that there is no limit to demand: demand is always going up."

"The sixth economic law of alchemy says that your immediate economic potential is defined by your technology gap."

"The technology gap is where you will find the greatest potential for growth. This is where the great majority of the Next Millionaires will come from in the years ahead of us."

"It has been only in the last hundred years or so that technology has begun to advance so rapidly. Now, all of a sudden, T is something that can change over the course of a single lifetime."

"Changes that used to take place in 50 years now happen in a handful of years…or even months. And how we deal with that changing technology explains almost everything."

"We're in the middle of a 'millionaire population explosion.'"

"Over the next ten years, we are poised to create an additional ten million-aires—raising the total number of U.S. millionaires to more than 18.5 million by 2016."

"Your work is defined by your skills and how well you keep pace with the dizzying rate of technological advance."

"Success in business depends largely on your adapting skills—the ability with which you learn new things."

"More than any other factor, how you manage your personal T today is what can make you one of the Next Millionaires tomorrow."

"How you get more technology is by improving your speed of communication."

"How much you discipline your mind to step out of its routines and look into new ways of doing things that you haven't yet adopted, is what will determine your economic potential."

"You cannot grow more hours in the day. However, you can make better use of those hours."

"You can no longer just pick a job and keep it for the rest of your life."

"By the end of this decade, the wellness industry will exceed $1 trillion."

"One of the most transforming effects of the Internet has been the empow-erment of the consumer."

"The #1 business opportunity for those who want to create new wealth is educating consumers about products and services that will improve their lives."

"Today, because technology is advancing so rapidly and making so many new products that can dramatically improve the quality of people's lives, if you are the one who tells them about that technology, you stand to make a fortune."

"The traditional wisdom in the second half of the twentieth century was this: go to school, get a good education, and go to work for a good company. The idea of 'going into business for yourself' was most often regarded as risky. Admirable, perhaps, but risky…and maybe a little crazy. Today, it's completely the other way around."

"We're in the midst of a boom in home-based businesses, and it shows no sign of slowing."

"The corporation has been decentralizing and dismantling itself, giving way to an environment of independent contractors."

"The greatest opportunities today are to go into business for yourself as an entrepreneur."

"Today, the real risk is staying with a large organization, because your job will probably be permanently dismantled within a few years."

"Congress has finally created a level playing field for individual entrepreneurs by creating tax laws that make it possible for entrepreneurs to enjoy the same benefits of tax-free or tax-deferred savings as employees of corporations."

"Now, individual entrepreneurs can actually get better health and retirement benefits than employees of large companies."

"Today more than 50 percent of Americans work either for themselves or for a small business."

"When you start your own business, you're going to put in the same hours as you did working for the corporation, if not more. But you get to control which hours."

"Of all the entrepreneurial opportunities available today, one of the most important is direct selling, also called 'network marketing.'"

"The direct selling industry is perfectly positioned to create many of these Next Millionaires."

"The direct selling community is a group that often picks up on trends long before the rest of the world has noticed them."

"The modern direct selling industry is poised to become the distribution method of choice for all new products and services."

"Direct selling is the perfect intellectual distribution business for today's economy."

"As powerful as the Internet is, it hasn't replaced the one-to-one, personal function of the modern direct seller, and it never will."

"The reason direct selling works so uniquely well is that a one-to-one personal conversation is virtually the only way we actively learn."

"Direct selling is the single most effective medium we have today, in the United States and around the world, for helping people close their technology gap."

"For most people, the only way you're ever going to accumulate a significant amount of wealth is through passive income."

"Direct selling provides an opportunity—open to absolutely anyone at all, regardless of background, specialized skills or accrued capital worth—to create a significant residual income."

"If you get involved in direct selling today, you are going to be exposed to trainings, materials, education, tools for developing belief systems and management systems that you're not likely to find anywhere else."

"You only win when you help others win."

"Economics is really a quest for happiness, a quest for recognition, for all those things that we really want, which money is a vehicle to acquire, achieve or attain."

"The act of being an entrepreneur is a theological act: it is a belief that God has given you the tools to go out, make money and take care of your family."

"People who make money and create wealth by owning and building their own businesses love other people."

"Direct selling is such a positive social and spiritual force in our culture right now because of its emphasis on inclusivity."

"Direct selling offers a very real solution to millions who stand to suffer from being on the wrong end of each technological shift."

"Business is about serving other people. The better you are at giving people something that improves their lives, the more successful you are, and the more money you make."

"Direct selling provides an unparalleled opportunity for millions of people to take responsibility for their own economic wellness, create long-term financial stability and even realize significant wealth, even while enriching the lives of untold numbers of others."

"At the core of your health is your diet: what you eat every day. And at the core of your wealth is your work: what you do every day."

"It's not just how many hours per week you put into your direct selling business that determines your income, but also how you use those hours."

"The most important factor that determines how successful you will be in direct selling is you."

"Beyond yourself, the three most important factors in your direct selling success are: the nature of the product or service, the strength of the company and its financial opportunity; and the particular team you will be working with."

"Here is the cardinal rule of direct selling: You should absolutely use and believe in the products or services you sell."

"Before you invest in anything else, exhaust the possibilities of investing in your own business first."

"The single most important trait for financial success is the capacity to willingly delay gratification."

About the Author

Paul Zane Pilzer is a world-renowned economist, a multimillionaire entrepreneur, a college professor and the author of five bestselling books.

Pilzer completed college in three years and received his MBA from Wharton in fifteen months at age 22. At age 24, he was appointed adjunct professor at New York University, where he taught for twenty consecutive years. While employed as Citibank's youngest officer at age 22 and its youngest vice president at age 25, Pilzer started several entrepreneurial businesses—earning his first $1 million before age 26 and his first $10 million before age 30. Over the last two decades, Pilzer has started and/or taken public five companies in the areas of software, education and financial services.

He was an appointed economic advisor in two Presidential administrations and warned of the impending $200 billion savings and loan crisis years before official Washington was willing to listen—a story that he later told in the book *Other People's Money*, which was critically acclaimed by *The New York Times* and *The Economist* magazine.

In *Unlimited Wealth,* Pilzer explains how we live in a world of unlimited physical resources because of rapidly advancing technology and how to prosper in this environment. After reading this book, the late Sam Walton, founder of Wal-Mart, said that he was "amazed at Pilzer's business capacity" and his "ability to put it into layman's terms." Pilzer's methods for predicting and managing technological change have been widely adopted by many of the world's leading corporations.

In *The Theology of Economics: God Wants You To Be Rich,* Pilzer explains how the foundation of our economic system is based on our religious heritage. This *New York Times* business bestseller was featured on the front page of *The Wall Street Journal* and on television shows ranging from *60 Minutes* to *First Person with Maria Shriver.* It has been published in 18 languages.

Pilzer's recent bestsellers, *The Next Trillion* and *The Wellness Revolution,* exposed our trillion-dollar food and medical industries and identified a newly emerging "wellness" industry that will soon occupy an additional one-seventh, or "next trillion," of our economy. In 2003, Pilzer was called the "wellness guru" on the front page of the Sunday *New York Times,* and in 2004, he received an honorary doctorate for his work in identifying and promoting the wellness industry.

A former commentator on *National Public Radio* and *CNN,* Professor Pilzer has appeared three times on the *Larry King Live!* television program and on the cover of several national magazines. He speaks live each year to tens of thousands of people, and more than 20 million audio and video copies of his speeches have been sold.

He lives with his wife and four children in Utah, where they are avid snowboarders, mountain bikers and chess players.

To learn more about Paul Zane Pilzer, please visit his Web site at www.PaulZanePilzer.com.

Paul Zane Pilzer Resources

You've read the book, now put your plan into action! Learn more about how to create a life of unlimited wealth with Paul Zane Pilzer's other resources!

The New Health Insurance Solution

Since 1945, most Americans have received health insurance directly from their employer. That is about to change. Employers are now telling millions of employees: "Go buy your own health insurance, and we will pay for it," or, "Here is up to $5,000, use it to pay for your basic medical expenses, and you get to keep any of that money you don't spend." The problem this book solves is that employees don't know what Health Savings Accounts are or how to buy their own health insurance, and they don't know how to shop intelligently for doctors, drugs or health care. Paul Zane Pilzer's book  explains to employees what their options are, why the new consumer-directed health plans are better, safer and cheaper than traditional employer-sponsored health insurance, and how the average family can save $5,000 a year or more on health care costs. *304-page hardcover book (Fall 2005 Release)*

The Wellness Revolution

How to make a fortune in the next big boom industry. Paul Zane Pilzer shows wellness professionals and entrepreneurs how to get in on the ground floor of the booming wellness industry. He predicts that within the next decade money spent on disease prevention will surpass that spent on disease treatment—and he shows readers how to stake their claim while there's still time. This insightful book shows how to take advantage of the wellness boom, but its lessons can be applied to any new market. *256-page hardcover book (paperback available)*

The Theology of Economics: God Wants You To Be Rich

Paul Zane Pilzer provides an original, provocative view of how to accumulate wealth and why doing so is beneficial to all of humankind. A theology of economics, this book explores why God wants each of us to be rich in every way—physically, emotionally and financially—and shows the way to prosperity, well-being and peace of mind. *288-page hardcover book (paperback available)*

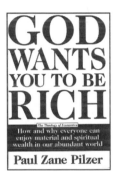

Unlimited Wealth

This is the book that started it all! Modern technology is transforming our most basic ideas about the creation of wealth. This book reveals how a new way of economic thinking is essential for success in today's world. Standing traditional economics on its head, Paul Zane Pilzer argues that the true problem is not lack of resources but a lack of demand. Technology has abolished resource scarcity and become the driving force shaping demand, economic wealth and progress. *226-page hardcover book (paperback available)*

Other People's Money

In his first book, Paul Zane Pilzer teamed up with Robert
Dietz, the business editor of the *Dallas Times Herald*, to
offer a hard-hitting, credible expose of the government
and private mismanagement and fraud that ushered in the
national S&L disaster in the mid-1980s. First offering a
concise history of the savings industry in the United
States, the authors went on to deplore its deregulation in
the '70s and '80s, arguing that this led to a virtually unlimited flow of brokered funds and risky investments by
incompetents and crooks. Accusing the Federal Home
Loan Bank Board of an extensive cover-up of such
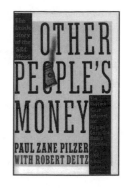
shenanigans, Pilzer and Deitz sensibly called for reform of the savings deposit
system, repayment of stolen savings to investors and incentives to restore our confidence in the virtue of thrift. *269-page hardcover book*

To order any of the books on these pages, please visit your favorite book reseller.

Ideal Prospecting Tools for Building Your Wellness Business

Join Paul Zane Pilzer and become a revolutionary for the cause of wellness!

The Next Trillion Audio

This live speech captures the rapid-fire passion of Paul Zane Pilzer as he shares his highly regarded wellness industry research. He explains that with Baby Boomers striving to feel better and live longer, healthier and more active lifestyles, they're going to spend significant sums of money on Wellness products and services. Get inspired as Pilzer lays out the irrefutable foundation for why the wellness industry is growing to more than $1 trillion and how you can build a profitable home-based wellness business. *Approximately 30 minutes*

The Next Trillion Book

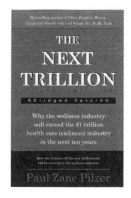

Written especially for direct sellers and network marketers! Paul Zane Pilzer shows why the wellness industry will exceed $1 trillion by the year 2010. He exposes the truth about why half the U.S. population is unhealthy and overweight. Learn why consumers will turn away from consuming more material goods and instead seek to achieve internal self-improvement. *The Next Trillion* offers an exhilarating vision of health and fitness—true wellness that is far more than skin deep. This is a critical must-read for entrepreneurs who want to know where the greatest opportunities lie ahead in the next two decades. *128-page paperback book*

Wellness Revolution Video

Wellness Revolution shows what's the next big thing—the $1 trillion wellness industry! Baby Boomers are striving to feel better and live longer, healthier and more active lifestyles; they're going to spend money on wellness products and services. This video presents and explains the options on how to profit from the exploding wellness marketplace! *Approximately 8 minutes*

To order any of these products, check with your company's tool supplier.